Breaking Away from the Corporate Model

Even More Lessons from Principal to Principal

Rocky Wallace

ROWMAN & LITTLEFIELD EDUCATION
A division of
ROWMAN & LITTLEFIELD PUBLISHERS, INC.
Lanham • New York • Toronto • Plymouth, UK

Published by Rowman & Littlefield Education
A division of Rowman & Littlefield Publishers, Inc.
A wholly owned subsidary of The Rowman & Littlefield Publishing Group, Inc.
4501 Forbes Boulevard, Suite 200, Lanham, Maryland 20706
http://www.rowmaneducation.com

Estover Road, Plymouth PL6 7PY, United Kingdom

British Library Cataloguing in Publication Information Available

Library of Congress Cataloging-in-Publication Data

Wallace, Rocky, 1956-
  Breaking away from the corporate model: even more lessons from principal to principal
/ Rocky Wallace.
     p. cm.
  Includes bibliographical references.
  ISBN 978-1-60709-431-9 (cloth : alk. paper) — ISBN 978-1-60709-432-6 (pbk. : alk.
paper) — ISBN 978-1-60709-433-3 (ebook)
  1. School improvement programs—United States. 2. School principals—United
States. 3. Servant leadership—United States. I. Title.
  LB2822.82.W355 2009
  371.2'07—dc22   2009027625

Printed in the United States of America

This book is dedicated to Barbara Walters and Imogene Wallace, my grand-mothers (who were also former schoolteachers); Randy Keeton; Dr. Bob Pearson; Dr. Debbie Wallace-Padgett; Charles "Chick" Thomas; Danny Knipp; Norma Meek; Rev. Mark Girard; and Rev. Fred Wiles, and to so many others who have crossed my path over the years and taken the time to mentor me. Life is about authentic, trusting relationships. These people invested in me something that meant far more than anything else they could have shared—they saw in me skills and talents that maybe I didn't realize I had, and they made sure I knew they cared. Thus, their teaching style ex-emplifies the underlying theme of this book: the relationship between the mentor and the pupil—the essence of teaching and learning.

Contents

~

Preface

In developing this *Principal to Principal* series, I have been blessed to have the opportunity to share the realities of what school leadership down in the trenches is really like. My graduate students and colleagues tell me that these stories speak to them and are very typical of what they experience every day. In defining the servant leadership model that is the cornerstone of this series, I am increasingly aware that too often principals, teachers, and students are being pulled toward the business of school and the mindset of endless production—often far away from the heart of school. This dangerous slide toward largeness and bureaucratic corporate models has put us in a perilous position, as large organizations who value profit over people typically find it difficult to rise above toxic and dysfunctional tendencies.

Here, in a simple story shared through the eyes of a principal and his mentor, I address this dilemma, illustrating a model that goes beyond brick-and-mortar solutions to heart-to-heart community and the fundamental need for simple, authentic mentor-pupil relationships. The true community school of the twenty-first century will look very different from past and even current traditional models, as socioeconomic barriers and other restraints force us to rethink the whole process of creating effective school structures.

Join me here in the exploration of new paradigms and fresh and unchained thinking, and in willingness to go back to the drawing board as we find ourselves at a critical stage in our culture's development, a crossroads that points down many possible paths. As educators, may we choose the better way. May we choose the path of service and authentic relationship. May we choose the path that leads home.

~

Acknowledgments

In my earlier books, I have acknowledged many colleagues and organizations who have so enriched my life and walked with me this path that has created such a wealth of rich ideas for stories about teaching and learning. None of this would be possible without the steady support and guidance of Dr. Tom Koerner and his serving staff at Rowman & Littlefield Education. So, to Tom and his talented crew, thank you!

And, what a joy it has been to serve at Morehead State University under the tutorage of our Dean of Education, Dr. Cathy Gunn, and the Chair of the Department of Professional Programs in Education, Dr. Wayne Willis.

There is one other key support group I must say "thank you" to as well. These are the people who know me best. These are the people who are there, no matter what the circumstances, day after day. This group is called, simply, my family. My wife, Denise; our girls, Lauren and Bethany; our parents; our siblings and their spouses; our nieces and nephews; our aunts and uncles; our cousins—this is my support group. This is the foundation that has mentored me, protected me, and supported me throughout my life. These roots run deep. These roots are "heart to heart." These roots are home.

CHAPTER ONE

~

A Simpler Time

> Schools should not be complex systems . . . the beauty of learning is its simplicity.

John was excited about his expanded role as a mentor to younger principals. After he retired two years earlier, his superintendent had talked him into working part-time with the other principals in the school district. John's program of small-group and one-to-one support to his colleagues down in the trenches had been so successful that he had been asked this year to help develop this pilot not just in his home district, but across the state.

One of John's new one-to-one assignments was with a principal of a small P–12 school in the next county, and as he drove up to the tiny campus, he thought to himself, "Just like the good old days." He reminisced about his own years in school and the little community that had nurtured him so well and prepared him for a good life.

"Hello, John. Come in and have a seat. Welcome to Smith School, named after one of our former superintendents in this county who was a legend back in his time. I was thrilled when the state called and said I had been assigned you as my mentor for this year. I've heard great things about your program and am so honored to be a part of it."

"You must be Mr. Williamson." John stretched out his hand and offered a warm and firm handshake. "Well, let me just say what a nostalgic walk back in time I took when I drove up to this school. I went to a little place like this, and I was blessed to have been surrounded by people who cared for me. School was more than where I went to learn every day. It was family."

"Call me Brad. Yes, we're definitely a throwback, John. But when the district was working on its new facilities plan a couple of years ago, this entire community pleaded for us to be allowed to continue as a preschool through high school center. With budgets as tight as they are these days, the school board looked at our track record of effectiveness and gave us its blessing."

"Well, I am certainly going to enjoy getting to know you and the nuances of this school, Brad. How many years have you been here?"

"This is my third as lead principal, and I was an assistant for a couple of years before that. I want you to meet my assistant, Millie, before you leave. She is new this year, but she does such a good job. I would like for her to sit in on some of our discussions, if that's okay."

"Sure! In fact, I'm forming a principals cohort for this region as part of this pilot project, and I'd love for both of you to be a part of it. We'll meet every few weeks, and this small group will be a great opportunity for you and Millie to share what's working here, as well as find out what some other folks are doing in their schools. Plus, it's wonderful to have a support group of fellow principals to talk to and to lean on."

"I'd love that, John. Thank you. There are times when this job gets rather lonely. Even though I have staff all around me, it feels as if I'm in a vacuum, and some days it's more like a fishbowl. And, I don't like taking my work stress home to my wife and the kids. So a cohort like this is just what the doctor ordered."

"Tell me more about your family, Brad."

"Oh, I'm so blessed, John. Angie, my wife, is a nurse at the regional medical center. We have two children. Paige is seven, and Barry is five. They are the joy of our lives!"

"I have been blessed too, Brad. Our kids are almost grown now, but Liz and I still do things with them all the time. Family is central to our lives, and I wouldn't have it any other way. In fact, the state department asked me to do a lot more traveling and staying overnight down state this year as we expand this mentoring program, but I just couldn't do it. I need my family, and they need me. So, I'm going to work this region, mainly, and keep the long trips to a minimum."

"When you were younger, just starting out as a principal, John, did you ever consider giving all of this up and changing professions? I find myself frustrated a lot with the whole process of 'school.' I feel like I run a good ship here. I'm good to the kids. I'm good to the staff and our parents. But sometimes, I just look around and ask myself if there is not a simpler way to provide the education these kids need. We do have a wonderful family atmo-sphere here, like you were describing earlier. But my teachers are exhausted way too much of the time with all of the bureaucratic stuff—you know, the endless paperwork, the test scores, mandates from above that sometimes just swallow us up and keep us from what we went to college to train to do."

"I did indeed ask myself those questions, Brad, off and on throughout my career. But what kept me coming back every year was that I knew I was mak-ing a difference. I knew the kids were thirsting for a school that cared about them. I knew my staff needed a shepherd they could trust. And I knew the town needed a community school it could be proud of. So, I stayed focused on trying to help our school be a model of excellence in a broken system. And ironically, that's why I'm now mentoring you younger guys and gals. It's your turn to stand in the gap and overcome the dysfunction. It's your turn to make a difference and create the model schools of the twenty-first century."

"That has an appeal to it, John. I need to hear more such pep talks!"

"Let me ask you something, Brad. A minute ago, you alluded to why you wanted to be a teacher in the first place. I'm going to push on you some here . . . why did you?"

Brad sat back in his chair, clasped his hands behind his head, and thought for a moment. "I went to college to learn how to help kids chase their dreams. One of my all-time favorite teachers, back when I was in fifth grade, inspired me so much about how fantastic school and learning could be. I am convinced she was the most important teacher I had in all those years from kindergarten to graduate school. She somehow connected with me—some-how could almost see inside me."

Brad's memory drifted far away, and he was now a young boy back in school. "Mrs. Daniels saw in me talent and potential that no one else had seen, except my parents. That's what I wanted to go into education for, John—to help kids go for it . . . fall in love with what they were finding out about their personal talents and the blessings of life, and go out there and make a difference . . . to find their passions, to chase their dreams."

"Don't you think you're getting to do that here at Smith School?"

"Some. But if we could somehow be given the freedom and resources to meet the developmental needs of each student, John, my oh my, what a school this could be."

"Sounds like you feel there is a gulf from here to there, Brad. You speak of what the school is, but then you have a wistful look on your face about what the school could be."

"You explain it well, John. And that's the frustration that is making me increasingly discontented."

"Thank you for being honest with me, Brad. I am going to enjoy our discussions this year. And if you'll just keep that restless tension inside focused on how to make the reality and the potential align, I can assure you this little school can be a model 'school of the future' that folks from far and wide will want to come and see. Do you believe this is possible?"

Brad felt something inside that said, "Trust this man. His insight may be just what you've been needing."

"School of the future? I like the sound of that, John."

Just then, Brad's assistant principal, Millie Thompson, came in with an urgent matter. John quickly introduced himself and made an appointment to chat further with both Brad and Millie the following Monday morning.

In *Strengthening the Heartbeat*, Thomas J. Sergiovanni (2005) takes us back to the heart of schooling—where values, not conflicting external expectations that scatter the vision, are the cornerstone.

Summary

Brad meets John, his new mentor, and shares that he's not sure how much longer he wants to work in the maddened pace of modern schooling. John speaks of a better way, and asks Brad if he would like to build a "school of the future."

Reflection:

1. Think back to one or two of your favorite teachers through the years. What made them unique?
2. How did they build authentic teacher-student relationships?
3. What barriers do you see today that tend to hinder a classroom's culture of community?

CHAPTER TWO

~

Black Swan

Wildcards can come out of nowhere, and in an instant, our best-laid plans are forever changed.

John was startled by his wife's urgent plea for him to wake up as he slept soundly in the hot August night. "What is it, Liz? Honey, I like to never got to sleep in this muggy weather. It's 1 o'clock on a Saturday morning—what on earth do you want?"

"It's the phone. Someone's trying to get in touch with you. Do you know anyone at a place called Smith School?"

"Yeah, that's where I was today. Why?"

"It's on fire."

John sprang out of bed and hurriedly put on a pair of jeans and a polo shirt. He raced to his truck and drove the thirty miles to Smithtown. The night sky near the town was lit up as if an Independence Day celebration was underway. As he arrived, John could see Brad standing near a fire truck, wearing khaki shorts, a white T-shirt, and a baseball cap. Several mixed groups of adults and youth were huddled together, quietly crying and consoling each other.

"It's gone, John. They think it may have been old wiring on the second floor. Nothing can be saved—not the gymnasium, not the elementary wing. Nothing."

"I'm so sorry, Brad. I came as soon as I heard. The main thing for you to do now is be there for your staff and the kids."

"And for the community. John, the school *was* this community. Practically everyone who lives here was served by this school at some point in their life. We had town meetings here. We had community suppers here. Groups of all kinds used this place—rummage sales, pie socials, you name it. The scouts met here, and the youth leagues used our gym and ball field out back. Basically, this was a school, community center, town hall, and YMCA all rolled into one. What you're seeing go up in smoke is not just an old school building. You're seeing Smithtown burning tonight."

As more and more people showed up, and the grieving could be heard above the crackling of old timbers, John realized what Brad had tried to explain. He knew Brad's people needed him, so he asked Brad if he'd like to meet later that morning for breakfast at a local restaurant. Brad nodded and patted John on the back. As John drove home, he felt as if he were playing a part in a movie. The night air and what he had just witnessed all seemed so surreal.

Later that morning, as Brad parked in front of the restaurant, John no longer saw the young man he'd met just a day before. Instead, he saw a much more mature man, burdened with the world on his shoulders, get out of his car and slowly make his way inside.

"What do we do, John? I'm to meet with our superintendent, Dr. Cobb, later this afternoon. Fall semester has already started, and the school district has absolutely zero space in any of the other schools."

"Son, just tell the super what's in your heart. Perhaps he's got an idea or two that would work for the rest of this school year. I wonder if he'd be willing to bus your students to neighboring counties until a new school can be built?"

"Yes, I thought of that. And I'm sure such a plan could at least be explored. But to be honest with you, the thought of Smith School being divided up and these kids absorbed and consolidated into several strange schools . . . , well, it will be such a jolt to this community. And it's already had its heart broken by the fire. These are good folk, John. This is farm country . . . with 'mom and pop,' family-owned businesses and a way of life that is small-town America through and through. For many of these people, their entire lives are wrapped up in what they've worked so hard to build here. Busting that up will cut deeper than can be measured."

"But what other choice is there, Brad?"

"You said to speak from the heart. So, I will. What I'd really like to propose to Dr. Cobb today would be for the community to house the school until the new one is built."

"What?"

"John, one of the pastors came to me last night as we all stood around watching the school burn, and he said his church would help in any way we needed. This morning, driving down here, I got to thinking. The simplest way for us to have school this year is to use the resources we already have here in Smithtown. We have about a hundred and fifty students in preschool through high school. The churches are set up with classroom space, parking, sanctuaries for student assemblies, and fellowship halls for meals. With the community helping, it would work, John!"

"How many churches are there here in Smithtown?"

"Three. I'd put our little ones and elementary-aged kids in one building, middle school in one, and high school in one. I know these people, John. They will do whatever it takes to keep their school, to keep their children right here in Smithtown."

"What will your superintendent say?"

"He's lived his whole life here. Besides, think how much money this will save him in transportation costs alone. And, how do we know that the schools in our neighboring counties will have enough room?"

"They probably won't. Most likely, they'll need to fix up some extra mobile units and just take on your kids and staff the best way they can. Plus, it could be that they won't need all of your staff. Some of your folks will probably be out of work."

"Then that settles it. I'm not going to let Smith School die, John. The old building may have burned up last night, but the spirit of the school, the heart of the school, was not destroyed. We can do this! Will you help me?"

"Son, I love your plan. And I love your devotion to your school and its community. Yes, I'm in. Let's do it."

In *The Black Swan*, Nassim Nicholas Taleb (2007) addresses the stark reality we must face when, out of nowhere, a chaotic event reshapes our world.

Summary

The entire Smithtown community is shaken by an early morning fire that destroys its school. As John comforts Brad in the aftermath, the young principal comes up with a solution so bold even John is taken back. Brad decides the best way to continue is to have the school housed in Smithtown's three churches.

Reflection:

1. Has a "black swan" circumstance ever happened in your school or community?
2. If you could reinvent your school, what are some nonnegotiables you would include?
3. What are the essentials that children and youth need from their school experience?

CHAPTER THREE

~

Paradigm Shift

There are better roads to travel—if we will leave the familiar trails we've walked for so long.

Brad's superintendent loved his ideas and asked for a special board meeting that Monday evening to get approval for what he called "The Smith School Project." The board embraced the concept as well, and Brad was given the green light to proceed. He asked John to join him in brainstorming with his staff to a hastily planned picnic at Brad's house that Tuesday evening.

Brad gave his staff the news. "Folks, here's the deal. We're going to have school this year, right here in Smithtown. And we're going to start a week from this coming Monday. So, we will have only missed two weeks. Our three churches here in town have volunteered their space over the next year or two until the new school is built, and our school board is taking care of any details this week and next to make sure we can have classes rolling without any further delays."

A murmur of mixed shock and excitement swept through the group. "Here's what we're going to do this evening," Brad continued. "Our new assistant principal, Mrs. Thompson, is going to take notes, and I need you to share your good ideas and also ask any questions you might have. As a team, we can do this. But, it's going to take us being creative and working together as never before. If our students and their parents see that we're excited and raring to go, then they will be just fine. But, if they perceive us as being flustered and in disarray, then they will lose confidence in us."

"I just want to know one thing, Mr. Williamson." A tall, veteran female teacher stood up from her lawn chair, spilling some of her tea. She was visibly shaken and upset. "Who in heaven's name ever dreamed up this wacky plan to have school this year in the first place? I mean, has anyone noticed that our building burned to the ground over the weekend?!"

Several others in attendance uttered approval of the frank comments. Some laughed, some clapped. Brad turned red, but kept his cool. "Well, Mrs. Petry, I was the person who asked our superintendent Saturday evening if he would consider letting us try keeping the school in the community. Otherwise, there was a real good chance we would have been forced to send our students to other districts outside this county. And as for your jobs, I'm not sure how that would have played out." The gathered faculty members looked at each other in dismay, now realizing the perilous situation Brad had been dealing with.

"One of our pastors offered his church, and the next thing I knew, the plan sounded too good to not at least try. So, we're here tonight to put our heads together and come up with a plan. This can be a horrendous year, or it can be a year of overcoming and doing something really special for this little town that we'll never forget. Basically, it's up to us—you, me, all of us—this staff team."

Others had questions. "What about meals?"

"What about ball games?"

"What about my room? I lost everything—Years and years of supplies! I'm not going to teach in a Sunday school room!"

Brad remained calm and just smiled as he answered each question. He was not mad at his staff. He knew they would need to vent and process.

"Our local restaurants are going to cater our food each day. Our various teams will play all their games on the road this year. And as for classrooms, all three churches are about the same size, and the way it works out, the three 'schools within the school' we used to have at the old building will simply each have their own space this year. Actually, there are advantages. Yes, your individual rooms will be smaller, but you're going to have volunteers coming in and helping from the community as never before. I've already been promised that we won't be on our own. Folks, we're going to be okay. I feel real good about this."

"But what about my science lab, Mr. Williamson?"

"And what about my band room?"

"And what about my home ec room?"

"And how will we run an ag program?"

"Oh, it will be a challenge, folks, no doubt. But each church has a large sanctuary that we've been told we can use throughout the week for the larger activities, and each church has a nice fellowship hall, too. Plus, the warm-weather months, there are outside pavilions, walking trails, and farms that connect to the church properties and there is plenty of room on the parking lots. What an opportunity for all of us to explore what it's like to start a school from scratch. What a chance to be as creative as you need to be."

"Mr. Williamson, won't the state stop us from doing this?"

"Actually, this is saving the powers that be from having to spend a whole lot of money on a very complicated plan. They are going to let us try this, no strings attached, almost like a charter school. In other words, people, you're being turned loose to experiment and teach the way you thought teaching was going to be when you were twenty years old back in college."

A young man who was just starting his second year spoke up. "How will you monitor three separate buildings?"

"Mrs. Thompson and I will work out a doable plan, I'm sure. Millie, do you have anything you want to add?"

The first-year assistant principal had sat off to the side in shock. She could not believe she had inherited such a bizarre set of circumstances in her very first year of school administration. But, as she listened to Brad, she had realized many positives she had not thought of over the weekend. "I just have one thing to add. We didn't choose to lose our school in a fire. But we can choose to make the best of a bad situation. I'm new, so I'll be learning right along with you all. I'm looking forward to it."

Brad could sense a calm coming over his staff, and he knew it was important to make sure any other issues were dealt with right now, before the group dispersed. "And let me add one option before we get to work tomorrow getting these three buildings ready for school. Dr. Cobb wanted me to convey to all of you that, if anyone just cannot handle this and wants to resign or retire, or wants help finding a job in another school in one of the surrounding counties, he understands. So, let me know as soon as possible if you want to move on."

No one said a word. No one nodded that they would consider the proposal. No one smirked. "I've always loved this staff, and I brag about you all the time. You're good at what you do, and our students are blessed to go to a school with such caring, talented teachers. And this year will be no different. We *will* have another great year—if we make that our unified vision."

Millie stood up and said, "Amen." And one by one, every person in attendance stood and joined her in smiling and clapping as they looked to Brad with trust and a collective determination that said, "We can do it."

...ge, John C. Maxwell (2003) shares the limitless
...g in new ways, maximizing intellectual capital that
...ly been untapped or overlooked.

Summary

Brad's bold plan is embraced by his superintendent and school board, and he shares the details with his staff. Despite their initial shock and some tough questions, they realize that what he has done may have saved some of their jobs, and they agree that as a team they will forge ahead.

Reflection:

1. Can you remember a time when bold change was implemented in your school?
2. Did the staff team rally around the cause with a unified vision and purpose?
3. If not, what has stopped innovative change from happening in your school community?

CHAPTER FOUR

~

Principals Cohort

*There is a soothing support that permeates through a band of shepherds,
creating a network that becomes a lifeline for protecting the flock.*

John asked Brad and Millie to join him that Friday at Hannigan Middle
School, where his principals cohort was meeting for lunch.

"Everyone, before we sit down to this delicious meal, I'd like to introduce
you to Brad Williamson and Millie Thompson. These are the two brave souls
who will be leading the Smith School project this year. I'm sure you've heard
and read about the fire, and the plan that has been put in place. Basically,
they're going to be piloting a brand-new concept in how to create a community school. Well, actually, it's not a new concept, but we've gotten away
from it over the years. We need to call Brad and Millie's staff the 'back to
the future' gang."

Everyone laughed, and John continued with introductions. He had six
lead principals and two assistant principals in this cohort, one of five such
support groups he was coordinating across the region. This was their first
meeting together, and he wanted to set the tone for the rest of the year. After
the meal, he led the discussion.

"Tell me, one at a time as we go around the circle, what is your greatest obstacle in doing your job as a school leader?" John knew he didn't need to talk too
much, so he gave the group plenty of time to reflect and share from the heart.

"I'll start." A plump, middle-aged man scooted his chair in closer. "I
thought I'd love being a principal. In fact, I couldn't wait to get my masters

in school administration and land my first job. But soon I realized it was not at all what it had looked like from the cheap seats. I feel like from my very first day at the helm, going on ten years now, I've never been caught up. I feel like my staff expects me to do more, central office expects me to do more, parents expect me to do more, and on top of those three groups, the state keeps piling new mandates on us every year."

He shook his head in frustration as he laughed at the irony and added, "And listen to who I just left out? The most important group we serve of all—our students. I try, but I will admit, I don't feel like I'm a very good principal. I tread water, maintain, survive. My blood pressure is too high, and in two years, as soon as I can walk out the door, I'm taking early retirement."

Others around the table nodded in agreement, and a young lady took her turn. "For me, personally, I get bogged down by all the distractions. I love the instructional leadership, and that's where I do the best work for my school. But to be honest, I don't get to that part of my job nearly as much as I should."

"I agree." A thin man with graying hair spoke up. "I would never have left the classroom if I had had any idea how overwhelming leading a school can be. I feel very much like a fireman. My wife even got me a fireman's helmet for Christmas last year, as a joke. What's so sad about it is that's exactly what I do every day."

Brad held up his hand for permission to speak. "I felt the same way, my friends. But ironically, after our fire last weekend, I now have a different focus. We're talking about survival this year at my school. The staff already knows that the petty stuff will have to cease. The kids know that they are lucky to not be bused to other counties. The community knows that it's going to take all of us—every day—to pull this off. And I know my role is to stand in the gap and keep pointing toward the vision of this year being a success as we march, so to speak, toward our new school."

Brad felt good, better than he had felt in a long, long time. The other principals looked at him with admiration, almost wistfully, as they wondered what it would be like to be in his shoes.

John transitioned to a second question. "Now, tell me what your greatest satisfaction is as you serve your school every day."

"Making a difference."

"Helping my school be a great place for kids to be."

"Helping solve the problems, however complicated, until we get to 'win, win.'"

"Providing support for my teachers so they can do their job in the classroom well."

Millie had not spoken yet, and she felt that she should contribute to the conversation. "This is my first year, and I know I have no idea yet what I've gotten myself into. But so far, these first few days on the job, I really love the many different ways every day I get to connect with people. I'm quiet, as Brad can tell you, and perhaps too shy. But I can already tell my passion is going to be in the relationships that I get to build all the time."

John smiled. "Millie, sometimes, the first days on the job, before all the clutter overwhelms us, can be our best. Why do you think that is?"

Millie thought for a moment. "Because I don't know enough about all the other parts of the job to be distracted yet? So, since I don't know what I don't know, so far I've just been trying to smile, be friendly, and help people when they call, e-mail, or come to my office."

John smiled again. "Well said, young lady. And what you are doing by instinct is what I had to get back to after my first couple of years at the helm, or I would have burned out and probably quit. I finally realized that my first responsibility to everyone who was depending on me to be a strong leader was to lead myself first. And a big part of that was identifying my own personal need to let go of trying to control all the clutter and instead see the bigger picture, which was, as you have explained so well, relationships."

John pointed his finger at the group with a fatherly smile and a word of caution. "To all of you, as soon as you can, have a 'heart to heart' with yourself, rediscover that passion you have for serving others, and then do that first every day. Before you know it, you'll start finding strategies that you had overlooked before to empower others to assist you in dealing with the distractions, freeing you up so you can be there for people—instead of being tossed to and fro as a ship on the sea."

Everyone sat still, and a hush came over the group. Finally, Brad spoke up. "John's right. I have realized over these last seven days that I had been spending too much time at my desk. Now, I have no desk. I had worried for weeks about how to move some classrooms around. Now, I have no classrooms. I had worried about how much it would cost to repair our copier. Now, I have no copier. I had worried about how to schedule equal practice time for our ball teams. Now, I have no gym."

Brad's eyes looked beyond the group, and he poured out what he had been feeling all week. "I had been spending too much time dwelling on trivial problems and minor issues and then taking them home. I now listen better than ever and provide support, but I don't take the problems home. I have realized this week, and I think my staff has too, that we had been spending too much time on the fringe instead of on the core purpose of why we even provide a school in our community. Perhaps we had lost our way. Our school

last Friday night, but in ten days our students are going
e will be teaching and learning in Smithtown. I've found
d it feels good."

In *The Courage to Teach*, Parker J. Palmer (2007) explores the very core of the teaching profession, challenging teachers to embrace true school reform by returning to the passions of the heart.

Summary

John's first session with his principals cohort exposes the feeling of being overwhelmed that many school leaders experience on a routine basis. Millie shares how her instinct to focus on building healthy relationships is proving effective, and Brad admits the reality of just how much of what he had been doing before the fire was trivial.

Reflection:

1. Are you currently, or have you in the past, been a part of a support or "think tank" group?
2. Why is the cohort concept important for those who work in stressful or isolated professions?
3. Has there been a time in your career when you felt disconnected from the passion of your work or the needs of your students?

CHAPTER FIVE

~

Opening Day

New beginnings have such vast potential to change our lives, to change our souls. We have but one obstacle standing in the way . . . our unbelief that we can indeed change.

John stopped by to chat with Brad the morning after Smithtown opened its new school. Brad was working at his computer in a makeshift office that had been a pastor's study at one time. But, with e-mail and other technology, the pastor now did his office work from home, leaving the space available for Brad.

"Come in, John! So glad to see you. By the way, Millie and I both thoroughly enjoyed the principals small group session. We both came away looking forward to our next meeting and realizing that we're not alone in this very unique world called the principalship."

"I felt sure you'd like it, Brad. I've not had one principal ever tell me they didn't need to reflect with other principals on the array of experiences and emotions that are all part of serving a school. Well, tell me, how did opening day go yesterday?"

"Oh my, what a 'moment in time' I'll never forget. I'll be telling my grandkids about it, I'm sure. Basically, John, it went very well. As I knew they would, this staff and the entire community rose to the occasion and have embraced the challenge of our task in the coming months. Bottom line—we trained adults and volunteers are here helping kids learn. In that regard, it's not that much different from what we were all trying to do down at the old building."

"Wonderful, Brad! I wanted to be here, but I was visiting a school a couple of hours away. They need lots of guidance in simplifying the entire structure and process so the school can be what it was meant to be."

"What are they struggling with?"

"The distractions."

"That's it?"

"Yep. It's really that simple. They have become so big, and everyone has so many theories for how to create a great school, that right now they are not even a good school. Their vision is scattered into various camps, all competing for the precious time that teachers have with their students."

"What are you going to suggest they do?"

"You may think I'm crazy, but later, I want to bring a team of staff from that school over here to observe your school."

"How's that?" Brad shifted in his chair, and his smile left his face. "John, how could we possibly be ready for visitors any time soon? You're joking, right?"

"Let me ask you, Brad—how did the master schedule feel yesterday?"

"It went well. I started here at the high school center, but I visited all three schools. Millie's office is at the middle school center, but she will go to the elementary in the afternoons on most days. All three school secretaries are now called office managers, and they are very good at what they do. All three sites ran without a hitch. I think the students were amazed at how pleasant and laid back the more intimate, smaller physical environment is. We certainly have no students getting lost in the back hallway, or not being able to find a classroom. And they're so much easier to monitor throughout the day. The staff has noticed a difference already."

"How did lunch go?"

"John, I never knew having meals brought in could be so smooth. With only fifty kids at each site, it doesn't take long to feed them, either."

"How did the after-school activities go?"

"Actually, our club sponsors and coaches, with the help of the community, are adjusting just fine. The ball field behind the old school is going to be adequate for outdoor practice, and the other student groups have the indoor room they need."

"What about your basketball and volleyball teams?"

"I knew you were going to ask. They're going to improvise, and they'll be okay. We've got outdoor courts around town, some in backyards. In cold weather, neighboring schools are going to free up some time for us during the season. Won't be like the good old days, with practice day and night and on weekends too, but you know what, John? Our kids are fine with it. They have realized that just the fact that we can still have school here in their hometown, and can still give them the opportunity to take part in an array of extracurricular activities, is pretty amazing in itself since the fire just happened two weeks ago. They've been real troopers about all of this, and they're adjusting well."

"What about technology?"

"All three churches have been upgraded by our district's technology team, and we have wireless laptops all over every center. Many of our students are bringing them from home. Each school has a business office, with the necessary technology to go with it. Again, with only fifty kids, it's not nearly as complicated."

"What about all the community groups who used your old building?"

"They're now using the churches later in the evenings and on Saturdays. The pastors love it! They say their buildings have come alive—all week long, for the first time, and not just on Sundays."

"How about bus schedules?"

"Interesting question, John. The superintendent wanted to use this opportunity to start over with *everything*. He's asking parents to transport their own kids as much as they can. Of course, buses are still running their routes, and we'll use them for field trips with students. But Dr. Cobb's philosophy is that here in the twenty-first century, perhaps there are some commonsense cost-cutting measures that we can glean from the fire that won't impede the educational process at all. He calls it his one year audit of 'the gravy train.'"

John smiled and nodded at the superintendent's bold embrace of forward thinking and simply said, "I like Dr. Cobb."

Brad's voice raised. "And let me tell you, he's leaving no stone unturned. If we can't show him it's being utilized as a key instructional tool with students, he's saying, 'Then maybe we don't need it after all.'"

"Good for him. Sounds like he's doing just what you and your staff are doing—letting go of some of the old deadweight as you build a brand new model. Must be exciting, Brad."

"Oh, it is, John. I feel like a new kid fresh out of college again. Did I tell you I'm teaching a life skills class with our juniors and seniors? We meet every Friday afternoon, and it's going to be a blast. I had not realized how much I missed the classroom."

"Wonderful! You see, Brad, this is exactly why I want to bring the school I mentioned earlier over here. They have all the brick and mortar, technology labs, gyms, and equipment they could ever need. But they are in many ways dysfunctional as a school. They need to throw away their old model, which doesn't work anymore, and start over."

"Well, I will say this, John. I had no idea how many things we were doing at the old building that were not really crucial for effective teaching and learning in the classroom."

reat work, Brad. See you Monday after next?"

ant to be here some when the students are all here, better
itments on Tuesdays from now on, John. We're going to a
four-day wₑₑₖ When the super said 'Let's start over,' we took him at his word.
We are confident that we can be just as effective by adding an hour a day and
freeing up Mondays for the staff and the kids to do field trips, club projects,
independent work, staff teams collaborating, some of the extra things that
are important, but don't work well crammed into the instructional day."

"And the state has approved this plan?"

"They are loving our commitment to simplify, John. With the fire and all,
we're being told to go for it. If we think it will be in the best interests of kids,
we're being given time to try it. Next year it may be different, but this year
we're being 'held harmless' to innovate as never before."

John just smiled and said, "Sweet."

In *Thinkertoys*, Michael Michalko (1991) offers insights into the world
of innovation and strategies for creative thinking, thus inviting the
mind to break free from the crippling habits of paradigm lock.

Summary

Smith School's new model brings with it a surprising simplicity that is flow-
ing much better than had first been expected. Brad shares with John several
examples of traditional bureaucracy and habits that have been converted or
discarded in favor of the essential priorities for creating an effective school.
John likes what he sees, and he asks if he may invite the staff from another
school he is working with to visit and to learn from the Smith School
model.

Reflection:

1. What paradigms or habits do you feel are still holding back the school
   of the twenty-first century?
2. What traditions that were needed in an earlier time are no longer logi-
   cal today?
3. Does your school encourage staff to visit model schools outside your
   own district?

CHAPTER SIX

~

Learning to Read

Before anyone can take off on a car trip, he must first learn how to drive. Before a child can fully explore the fascinating world of learning, he must first learn how to read.

John was anxious to visit with Brad again, as he wanted to know more about this concept of reinventing the entire schooling process. As a principal years earlier, he had often wondered why some practices that were ineffective were so ingrained in the traditional culture of school. It was mid-September, and he was planning his quarterly time away with his family.

"I'll be gone the first week in October, Brad, so if you wish, let's meet both this week and next week."

"Works for me. Where are you running off to, John?"

"Taking Liz and the kids for a week of camping, hiking, and sightseeing. We do a vacation of some kind every quarter, and we've grown to love this family tradition."

"Sounds wonderful, John. But how can you afford it? And how can you all synchronize your calendars to pull this off?"

"Actually, Brad, we can't afford not to do it—that's how much it means to all of us to slow down and soak in this precious time together. And we adjust our calendars just like you all here have adjusted your calendar. I've learned over the years that when something's a priority, I can find a way to get it done."

"I love the concept, John. As a matter of fact, I'm going to talk to Angie about this. Paige and Barry are little still, but they'll grow so fast. What memories they would have later on!"

"We're blessed, Brad, to have the families we get to go home to every day. I sometimes still pinch myself that I get to live this life that I've been given. I never want to take it for granted. And I want to give back by serving and making a difference. Once I figured it out, that this is the least I can do, so many answers to life's other questions fell right into place."

"I agree, John. And may we never forget—so, so many folks who we assume are doing okay are not. So the opportunities to serve will always be there. Just this morning, one of our freshmen here, Andrew Lawson, came to me and said he was quitting school. I counseled him and tried everything I could think of to get him to give us another chance, but his mind is pretty much made up. He's coming back in tomorrow to see me one last time." Brad seemed defeated. "What do you do in a case like this? His folks are split up, his mom works two jobs just to make ends meet, they live in a run-down little shack that's way too small for a household of kids. Andrew will have a rough, rough go of it, I'm afraid. I would do anything to keep him here—this is his 'hiding place.' This school is his only hope of escaping the cycle he's been born into, a dark hole so many kids like him don't seem to be able to climb out of."

"Are you serious when you say you would do anything, Brad?"

"What do you mean?"

"Why is Andrew quitting? What do your teachers say?"

"Bottom line, John? He can't read."

"So school, for him, is part of the dark hole you just spoke about."

"When you consider the fact that he can't read, I guess it's not the safe haven for him that it is for most of the other kids, John."

"So, tell me, Brad, what are you going to do about it? Tomorrow, he walks away. Tomorrow, Andrew says goodbye, and once he walks out the front door of this school, you'll never see him again."

"What would you do, John? Because, to be frank, I've probably got a few more Andrews, already fallen through the cracks but disguising their academic struggles and pretending everything is just fine."

"What would I do? If I was sitting on top of one of the boldest experiments in education that this state has seen in decades? Well, first of all, that would be my leverage. I'd take this entire fall term and methodically peel back the outer covering of every classroom in this school, one by one, all the way down to preschool, and I'd make reading first."

"Reading first?"

"Indeed. I'd make sure every teacher, every aide, every volunteer, every student was reintroduced to the foundation of learning—which, simply put, is being able to read well."

"But John, even with our small class sizes, we don't have the resources to do what you suggest."

"Really? I thought you told me this entire town was committed to this school, Brad? These three centers, with these one hundred and fifty students, could be transformed if you had volunteer mentors who would come in for an hour or two a day and help your staff teach every child to read."

"I never thought of it like that before, John. I just never pictured asking lay people to work with kids in reading. It seems a bit much to me."

"Do you have any lay people helping with your ball teams or student clubs?"

"Sure."

"Then why would you not want to tap into the wealth of human resources in this community and put them right here in the school as reading buddies for your kids?"

"I don't know. For one thing, our rooms are too small."

"What about all that space upstairs in the sanctuary? What about the fellowship hall? What about the hallways? In warm weather, what about outside?"

"Makes sense, John. Actually, it makes too much sense. That's probably why we've never tried it."

John laughed in agreement. "How many kids in all three buildings do you think need extra tutoring in reading, Brad?"

"I'm guessing twenty percent."

"OK. That's thirty kids. Not counting your teachers and aides, how many additional volunteers would you need?"

"I'd be thrilled with ten."

"Would your staff work with you and help train them?"

"You know what the super said. This year, we're starting over with everything. I don't think anyone would buck it, John. They might be a little squeamish about it at first, but I see what you're getting at. We've got untapped human resource capital right here in Smithtown, people who want this school to succeed, who want the children of this community to do well in school and do well in life. I can find ten volunteers to help us reinvent our reading program. Maybe fifteen or twenty. And it won't take that long to get it started. Why would we let one child move on from grade to grade, not knowing how to read? When you look at it that way, it's madness."

ew? In less than twenty-four hours, he's gone."

n in mind for Andrew, John—a retired teacher

ιer day and told me she'd help us out part-time if

 Dr. Cobb on this one. I bet when he hears what

ᵗind a way to pay her to help me coordinate this

̲ ̲ ̲ ̲ ̲ ̲ ̲ but ner first responsibility will be to work with Andrew, every morning, all year. But do you think Andrew will stay in school, or is it too late?"

"I think if you can introduce Andrew to this mentor tomorrow, and she connects with him as someone who really cares and who will help him out of that black hole you talked about, he'll give it a try, Brad, for a few days at least. You might need to do some bartering with him, too."

"Bartering?"

"Yes, you know—in return for him not divorcing the school, you find him a job or responsibility that he would love and take great satisfaction in doing for the school."

"Well, I do know he loves hunting, fishing, anything involving the out-doors."

"Do you have a club going that fits that description?"

"No, but guess what, John? I just started one right now. And I know who would volunteer to sponsor it for us. I'll call him in a few minutes."

John stood up to leave, and Brad cut him off at the door. As they shook hands, Brad said "Thanks, John. You helped me see something I had not been able to see before. You may have saved Andrew, and dozens more like him over the next few months and years."

In *The Schools Our Children Deserve*, Alfie Kohn (1999) challenges the education profession to look beyond tradition to create effective learning centers that focus on how and why students learn.

Summary

As Brad bemoans the fact that he is losing a student who is dropping out of school because he can't read, John challenges him to do something about it. As the two discuss the reality that there are several more Smith School kids who can't read, Brad decides to make changes to prevent any of his students from slipping through the cracks without this critical learning skill.

Reflection:

1. Have you ever been frustrated that the system seems to rush you when you have students who need more intensive help with reading skills?
2. What strategies are in place in your school to ensure that all students are reading well before they move on to the next school?
3. Does your school recruit and train volunteer tutors to help students in reading?

CHAPTER SEVEN

~

Lifeline

*My friend was there to listen, not judge, and reminded me that we all
have issues. I soon learned to see myself more honestly, and to then accept others joyfully, without concern for their imperfections.*

Brad and Millie had been looking forward to the next principals cohort
gathering and they had several questions they wanted to ask other principals
about what was working well in their schools. But as John started the discussion, a young man who had not been at the first meeting interrupted with
tears in his eyes and a quivering voice. "I can't do this anymore."

John immediately played down any awkwardness and postponed his first
question. "Go ahead, Rudy. I think we've all been there. Tell us what's going
on, and we'll listen."

"Well, this is my second year. I realized last fall when I took the job at my
school that I was not really cut out for supervising other adults. But I didn't
quit; I thought that maybe some of it was just the rookie jitters, and I tied a
knot in the rope and hung on until the end of the school year. I went to every
conference I could attend this past summer, and I had a lot of self-confidence
when my staff and the students returned to school this fall. But, I've had it.
I have a very strong-willed staff, and they bicker and disagree on so many
things. They don't seem to like me, and I don't enjoy refereeing their petty
immaturity all the time. It's just a terrible match. I just want to go back to
the classroom."

John was kind, as he realized this one issue of employee discontent was what kept most leaders up at night more than anything else. "Tell me, Rudy, do you like the other aspects of being a principal?"

"For the most part, I do, John. Oh, it has its ups and downs, and I never feel caught up, but I do think our school is making steady progress, and I do think I'm building good relationships with the kids and their parents. The community is very supportive, and our central office is very supportive."

"Son, it sounds to me like you're being too hard on yourself. If you have your school headed in such a positive direction, are you sure you want to quit?"

"John, I don't like babysitting other adults. It's that simple. I've got some staff that keep my kettle hot, if you know what I mean. It never ends. For example, just the other day, one of my janitors called in sick just before he was supposed to show up for his shift. How was I supposed to find a sub on such short notice?"

"Do you think he did that on purpose?"

"No, he went to the hospital later with a gall bladder attack. But, surely he knew earlier in the day that he wouldn't be able to make it in to work that afternoon."

"Maybe, maybe not."

"Here's another example. Last week, I was right in the middle of explaining our new math program in a faculty meeting, when suddenly one of my veteran teachers started ranting and raving about not having time to digest all that we were doing this year. It totally ruined the tone of the meeting."

"Had you discussed this possible addition to the curriculum with her ahead of time?"

"Well, no. But John, she's a grown woman."

"Yes, a grown woman with tremendous stress on her every day to perform miracles in her classroom."

"What are you saying, John? That these incidents are my fault? Here's my most recent nonsense. As I was leaving my school this morning for this cohort, I met one of my new teachers in the parking lot. Apparently, she had overslept. But had she called me to explain? No-o-o-o. She was trying to slip in and slide right down the hall to her room twenty minutes late. I can only hope her aide was in that classroom watching the kids."

"You're right, Rudy. She should have called and made sure her room was covered. Maybe she did, but she failed to contact you, too."

"And John, this is not the half of it. I have a couple of teachers who don't like each other, and everyone in the building knows it. They won't even sit at the same table at lunch or talk with each other in a staff meeting. It's absolutely ridiculous. I could go on with other examples, but you get the point."

"Seems to me, Rudy, that all of these are examples of staff perhaps needing some training in emotional intelligence."

"What's that?"

"Basically, it's the ability all of us have to improve our relationships with others—our listening skills; our ability to see the other person's perspective, read the situation, know what to say and when to say it to help the other person to feel affirmed and respected."

"You mean the staff would have fewer bumps in the road if we went back to the basics of how to treat others? Never thought of it much, but I would have to agree, John."

"Exactly. How can we expect our educators to build good relationships with students and parents if they can't even get long with their colleagues or their principal? And it goes both ways, Rudy. We principals too often carry way too much baggage around, making us like time bombs ready to go off. The least little thing, and we assume someone is mad at us or out to get us. Partly due to the stress of running a classroom and a school, educators' emotions typically run high. But it's not healthy for any staff team to not have good, trusting relationships. As goes this one variable, so goes the school."

"I see your point, John. So tell me, how do I set up such training? And how do I get my staff to buy into it? Won't they laugh me out of town on this one?"

"Actually, if you run this by your school council, and work in small doses of it as bonus training in teachers' meetings, that would be a great way to start. Then, as time goes on, you could expand it to all of your staff teams, including you and your office team. As a matter of fact, if I were you, I'd start with your office first. That way, you're modeling for everyone else."

"Do you have a recommendation for who to contact to help us with this?"

"Actually, I have just the school. Last year, I worked with the principal over at Blue Creek High School, and his school culture is very strong—largely due to his learning to model servant leadership. His entire staff and school community picked up on this philosophy, and the result is very impressive. It transformed the school. If it's okay with you, I'll contact the principal, Todd. Perhaps you and he could visit each other's schools, and do some one-to-one time this year, much like we do in this small group. I know Todd would help."

"I'd like that, John. Could you, Todd, and I perhaps have lunch sometime soon?"

"Sure thing. I'll set it up."

at a Higher Level, Ken Blanchard (2007) details a comprehensive step-by-step plan for empowering and equipping individuals
and organizations to be models of authentic leadership.

Summary

A young principal breaks down during a cohort session, sharing the frustra-
tions he is having with the adults he supervises in his school. John suggests
that he spend some time with Todd, whom he had helped the previous year
to address relationship issues.

Reflection:

1. Do you have a mentor or accountability partner?
2. Does your school have a staff development model that includes one-to-
   one mentoring, at least for new teachers in their first two years?
3. Has your staff had any training in the domain of emotional intelligence?

CHAPTER EIGHT

~

"My Kid Can't Do Math"

While on vacation with his family, a little boy was visiting a famous statesman, who had been recognized throughout his career as a renaissance man, seemingly adept in anything he tried. "Sir, how did you get so smart?" the little boy asked. The older man thought long and hard about how he had acquired his many skills, then replied, "Reading and math, son. In the beginning, my parents and my teachers would not let me get by without learning everything I could about reading and math."

John was surprised to get a phone call from Brad that same evening, and he called him back as soon as he got the message. "John, on our way back to school today, Millie opened up to me and shared some things that I need your advice about. I know tomorrow's Saturday, but would you have some time in the morning to meet me somewhere to talk?"

"Sure, Brad. Want to join me on a hike? I'm heading out to a favorite trail of mine with my camera around daybreak, and I would love to have you tag along."

"How early?"

John laughed. "How about if I meet you at the grocery store at the county line at seven A.M., and I'll drive from there."

"Okay, I can handle that, I think. See you then."

John had picked up this hobby a couple of years before he retired, and he loved to explore new trails. Often, he took his kids with him, but today they all had plans, so he was glad that Brad could come along. As the two made their way down a beautiful country road that meandered through thick woods, Brad opened up. "Millie's really upset, John."

"I thought she seemed extra quiet at our group session yesterday. What's wrong?"

"A couple of things. One of our veteran teachers jumped her this week about all of the new ways we're doing things this year. It seems we have a small group of teachers who do not like all of the volunteers being recruited to help with reading."

"Well, you're not really surprised that there is some resistance, are you?"

"No, but I don't appreciate a teacher going around me and trying to intimidate my assistant principal, who is brand new this year. Millie is doing a very good job, and I don't need her distracted by a lot of emotional stuff from staff."

"Brad, you know what?"

"What?"

"I learned after my early years of leading a school that the vast majority of the issues I was asked to fix were emotional stuff. Is Millie one who runs from confrontation?"

"Yes, like the plague."

"Then, over time, this job will eat her alive. Tell you what let's do. You know the training on emotional intelligence that I was explaining to Rudy yesterday?"

"Yes. And I was impressed, too. You think I should build some of that in at Smith School?"

"Yes. But why don't you focus more on building a protocol for all of your staff so they know it's okay to vent and actually good to lay their concerns on the table. As this 'reinventing school' experiment unfolds, the more input you can have from others on the detailed decisions, the better."

John thought for a moment, then a gleam came to his eye. "Why don't we do an after-school session for all of your staff, from all three centers, on how to agree to disagree agreeably, and then on a regular basis build in some follow-up? Most teams in organizations don't do a very good job of making group decisions in a healthy way. This could be a huge shot in the arm for Smith School, especially with so many volunteers from the community involved. In reality, everyone who helps with the school in any way needs this training sometime this fall."

"Will you help me with this, John? Would you introduce what you've just explained here during my next teachers meeting and outline for us how to integrate it with all of the people who serve Smith School?"

"Yes, I'd be glad to, Brad. It's so futile for your stakeholders to agree on the surface, but then be fuming behind the scenes. That builds distrust, creates a toxic culture, and weakens the momentum of the organization. You tell Millie help is on the way. I'm glad she brought this up—you'll notice a big difference."

"Now to her other issue, John. One of our most supportive parents came in this week and jumped all over Millie about our math program. She said her daughter needed a scholarship of some kind if she was going to go on to college and that she had scored terribly on the math section of her ACT. Millie calmed her down and told her she'd look into it. When she looked at our over all student ACT scores in recent years, math stood out as our weak-est content area. What I'm trying to say is, the mother had a good point. What do I do?"

"Well, first of all, don't think this is a problem unique to Smithtown. All over the country, kids typically score lower in math. It's an issue that has gotten the attention of many from various circles, and increased demand is going to be placed on schools to learn how to teach math more effectively. What do your high school math teachers say?"

"They say that foundational principles aren't being covered thoroughly enough in the earlier grades. And they blame the pressure to cover too much material in a short amount of time to get ready for state and national assess-ments each spring."

"What do you think, Brad? Do all of your teachers, elementary through high school, know how to teach math well?"

"No. Some do, but some avoid the more advanced math."

"So your problem is twofold. For starters, some of your staff don't truly have the expertise. But also, there's a lot of exterior pressure that is assess-ment related—so, in reality, this type of external accountability probably hurts some of your students more than it helps."

"Yes, you've nailed it. So what do I do?"

"I'd say, first of all, you need to find a way to bring together all of your teachers who work with students in math concepts of any kind and have a very open discussion about where the learning gaps are. Show them the ACT results over the last several years. Then, let them develop a corrective action plan for Smith School's entire math program, from preschool to primary, to intermediate, to middle school, to high school."

"I can do this, John, but you know what they'll say. They need more train-ing, they need more time, and they need less stress piled on from the state and the feds demanding that they cram in too much material each year."

"And Brad, they will be exactly right. Listen to them, and be supportive by helping them with all three requests. The superintendent is going to give you the increased training you ask for, I guarantee it. He knows as well as any of us that there have to be changes in how we help kids to grasp math concepts. And the need for your teachers to have more time to work together in finding solutions to these gaps can be resolved with your Monday schedule, when the students aren't at school. Why can't your teachers revolutionize your math program by making it their Monday project for the rest of the year?"

"Good point. They can."

"And as to the outside pressure to cover vast amounts of material and to meet all of these assessment requirements? I promise you, if you do these first two parts well—more math training for your staff and more common time for them to meet and discuss student work and student needs, number three will fall right into place. But also, tell your teachers to teach math with depth and quality, which means they will have to let some things go. Do you know what our athletic coaches do that we all could learn from in our other classrooms?"

"What's that?"

"They stress, over and over, the basics. They work on fundamentals day after day—the same drills, same repetitions, until the players can do most of it in their sleep. Just as in reading, Brad, we've lost our way a bit in how we teach math. We've compromised quality for quantity."

"And I'm going to do something else, too, John. I'm going to recruit some volunteers who have worked in careers that required strong math skills to help us with all of this. I know there are at least a few in this community who could tutor kids in small groups and one on one and really make a difference."

"Great idea, Brad. I'm going to tell you a story, a sad, but true story. I have a cousin who to this day has scars from the very dilemma we have been talking about. Her dream, all the way back to when she was in grade school, was to be a doctor. And when she graduated from high school, she kept chasing that dream. She went on to college and majored in pre-med. But all the way through school, she was never able to do very well in her math courses. Finally, being rejected time and again from med school, she finally gave up on her dream, and settled for an entirely different field."

"What happened to her?"

"Oh, she's lived a good life, done well, raised a great family, and is now putting her own kids through college. But when I ran into her at a family reunion a while back, she had a sadness in her voice as she told me that when she noticed her kids having trouble with math, she hired a math tutor for herself so she could learn how to teach them what they needed to know."

"Did it work?"

"Sure it did. Her two oldest are in college now, both majoring in fields that will require some math expertise. And they're excelling. She just looked at me and said, 'John, all I needed was someone to take the time to tutor me. This second time around, after years away from the classroom, I picked up the concepts in a snap. It finally clicked. But no one had been able to show me before.'"

"And you think, John, she really would have been a doctor?"

"I have no doubt in my mind, Brad. She's one of the brightest, most self-disciplined people I've ever known. She would have excelled, if she could have just made it over that first hurdle."

"I wonder how many others we are letting down like this, although we're trying hard?"

"Too many."

"And I wonder if the lack of ongoing conversations between parents and teachers don't make a larger difference than we used to think. We are realizing that even in a small-school atmosphere like this, way too many parents are not in relationship with our school."

"In relationship? I like what you're getting at, Brad. Tell me more."

"You know—not emotionally tied to us except to attend school events their children take part in. I'm wondering if we should not require much more one-to-one parent-teacher conferencing, perhaps a minimum of at least once every quarter. With our flexibility on Mondays and our focus on reinvention, what would be the downside to this?"

"There is no downside, Brad. Imagine how much stronger this school would be if all parents were engaged with their children's learning, or at least were more aware of what is needed to have their kids truly well prepared for a life of fulfillment."

"John, this idea is exciting. It's so packed with potential. If we could implement this and stay with it, we would truly be internalizing the real meaning of community school."

"So, what's stopping you, Brad? Perhaps the realization that some parents, and some teachers, will say this is not needed?"

"Yep. Our naysayers will cry about how much more work this is. But you know what? Our Monday time is our ace in the hole on this, John. We have no excuses."

"So what are you going to do, then?"

"I'm going to do it. From now on, parent conferences and our relationships with parents are no longer something we dance around as if it's not a critical piece for any authentic, relationship-driven school. We're going to address it, we're going to develop strategies in team meetings, we're going to rethink why we are not tapping into this resource we have at our fingertips—the parents of our students. And part of the plan will be that we're going to hold

ـ

35

,untable. Some of them see us as a babysitting service. ,ols exist, and we need to change that mindset."

through and be relentless about it, this school will never
"

"Λι en't we glad about that! It's time, my friend, for this staff team, and paι ts too, to step up as never before. In fact, it's past time."

In *Creating We*, Judith E. Glaser (2007) challenges organizations to break free from the paralyzing, self-focused habits of the past and create a culture of problem solving by using human capital in smarter, more effective ways.

Summary

Brad's assistant principal, Millie, is frustrated with the petty issues that keep staff emotional and distracted, and also with the school's poor ACT scores in math. Brad develops a plan that will tap into volunteer math tutors from the community. He and John also zero in on the potential of the Monday flex time to allow teachers to build strong relationships with parents, while also holding parents accountable to get more involved with their children's learning.

Reflection:

1. Does your school recruit and train volunteer tutors to assist students in math?
2. How does your school build parent conferencing into blocks of time that are convenient for both staff and parents?
3. How does your school train parents to be more accountable for their children's learning?

CHAPTER NINE

Life Skills

Before living a principled life that is fulfilling and productive, one must know what such a purposeful journey looks like.

John met with Brad's staff during their next faculty meeting and introduced them to the current research on emotional intelligence. They were fascinated; some had never heard the term before. John told them to just shorten it to EI, and to remember that if they worked on their EI in every encounter throughout the school day, whether with students, parents, or other staff, they would start seeing a positive difference in all three school centers. Brad had already begun discussing with staff the need to hold parents accountable by requiring routine parent conferences on Mondays, and John worked this into his training seamlessly, stressing that relationship is key.

John also scheduled a follow-up visit for the next week so the staff could discuss EI further and begin to work on what it means to be a member of a healthy team. The response to the idea of learning how high-performing teams work was mixed. Some were excited, some sat with their arms crossed, and a few mumbled under their breath while John was talking. After being with them for only a few minutes, he knew this group needed this training. After the meeting, he went with Brad to his office to see how things were going over all.

"It's been a very smooth first semester, John. I am so proud of this staff, the kids, the community—everyone has pitched in and made this work.

And it's an effective model. I love the simplicity and the family atmosphere. Our discipline referrals are down, our after-school detentions are down, our student and staff attendance is up, and the teachers indicate that the student work in the classroom is more focused. I would have never dreamed we'd see so many positives so soon. I have, though, noticed a huge gap while teaching my life skills course to our upperclassmen."

"What kind of gap?"

"They need an old-fashioned dose of common sense."

John chuckled and nodded his head in agreement. "I knew you were going to say that. Are you finding that they are so locked in to their personal interests that they sometimes seem to be oblivious to the world around them?"

"Well, yes, that too. But John, I'm talking about the basics of survival as they get ready to leave our nest here and transition out into a great big world out there. I've been doing some surveying of their needs so I could make this course relevant to them this year. What I'm finding out is that these kids need to know how to write letters as they start filling out college applications. No, let me correct that—they need to know how to complete application forms, period, whether it be for school, employment, whatever."

Brad seemed frustrated, at a loss for the right words to make clear to John the extent of this critical learning gap. "Many of them don't have time management or good study habits. And they need basic math skills for everyday life, such as balancing a checkbook or doing mental math as they stand in a store and compare prices. They seem not to know how to do math in their heads at all."

Brad paused, as if to say, "I'm feeling a little overwhelmed with this, and I've just started the course." He went on aloud, "And some of them have requested that I spend some time on social skills, as they feel ill-equipped to carry on relaxing conversations with adults. In fact, some want to study more about what it's like to be an adult—what it takes to do well in college or in their first job, buying a house, getting married, having children, building a career. And I've had a couple who say they need to know more about how to avoid alcohol and drug abuse, as they have friends who are inviting them to take part in some weekend activities they aren't sure will be drug free.

"And it's not just the risky stuff, John. Many of these kids are not taking care of themselves in the day-to-day routine. They don't exercise enough, they don't eat well, and they don't sleep much. They don't understand the basics of good health. In some ways, it baffles me, because they should know better. And the list goes on, John. I've just mentioned a few examples."

John replied, "I commend you, Brad, for beginning this new course by asking your students what they needed that was most relevant to them. We need to be doing more of these types of student interviews and letting the kids plan with us so we can be operating more effective schools—smart schools—I like to call them. To get back to your dilemma: a couple of other schools I've visited recently have top-notch advisor-advisee programs that they have committed a lot of careful planning and resources to."

"Yes, we have tried that here in the past, but it seems to depend on how well the homeroom teachers buy into it, and then use the time wisely. But, to be honest, we've not paid enough attention to the structure. So I'm sure the kids, and some of the teachers, have seen it as a lightweight program that is not very important to our overall menu of services."

"But it is important, Brad. Based on what you've just told me, it's of critical importance. You mentioned that the students seem not to have an abundance of common sense. But, think about it. Who has been modeling for them all of these years they've been in school? Us! I'm going to push on you some here: what's gotten in the way of our common sense?"

"What do you mean?"

"I'm just saying, Brad, we know what our upperclassmen need to have a good handle on as they move on from here into young adult life. So why do we tiptoe around these basics and then whine about the fact that our kids aren't prepared to be productive citizens? Shouldn't we, the education community, be the first to step in with a more varied and prioritized curriculum that does get them ready for life? After all, isn't that what their parents and the larger society are all assuming we're doing when we have these kids, counting preschool, for fourteen years?"

"You're right one hundred and ten percent, John. But what do you suggest I do?"

"Does Millie help with this life skills class?"

"No, she's at one of the other school centers in the afternoons most of the time."

"But could she help you develop a high quality advisor-advisee program for this school? You could still reinforce these gaps we've been talking about in your Friday afternoon sessions, but it sounds to me that all of your high school teachers need to be helping on this project. In fact, your middle school needs to be built into this model, too."

"Millie loves to be assigned projects like this, John. And she's thorough, too. Great idea."

"And, I could give her the names of the other schools I mentioned, so she could do some research on how they have built advisor-advisee into their master schedule so that it's an integral part of the total curriculum, not just a glorified study hall."

"I like it, John. Let's do it."

In *Five Minds for the Future*, Howard Gardner (2006) describes the skills that the student of the future will need, skills that transport the learner of the twenty-first century far beyond the traditional limited curriculum of the past.

Summary

As Brad works with upperclassmen in his life skills class, he realizes that they do not have a grasp of basic knowledge they will need as they transition to the next stage of life after high school. He and John discuss the advantages of adding an advisor-advisee program to the school's menu of services, as John has observed this concept working well in other schools.

Reflection:

1. Does your school have an advisor-advisee program? If you work with younger students, what is your school's process for making time for teaching life skills?
2. Do you as a staff team intentionally build life skills into the total curriculum and menu of services?
3. Think of an example in your life or with your own children where you discovered a gap, a key concept that one would have expected to be covered at some point in school.

CHAPTER TEN

~

They're Still Kids!

She awoke early in the morning darkness . . . still just a child, but feeling as if the world was on her shoulders.

November was here, and the holiday season was just around the corner. Brad had followed John's lead and taken his family on a three-day weekend to the mountains, and he was bubbling over with how much the time away had been so good for all of them. But his tone changed when Millie stuck her head in the door and interrupted his Tuesday morning time with John.

"I hate to barge in guys, but I've got a situation on my hands. Billy Oates, our ace on the middle school academic team, just walked out of class and said he's going home. I'm going to get him, but I wondered if you all would let me bring him in here and try to help him get whatever it is off his chest."

Brad nodded his head in agreement. "Sure thing, Millie. Go get him, and let's see what's going on."

In about twenty minutes, Millie returned with Billy. It was obvious he had been crying.

"What's wrong, Bill?" Brad had known the boy for years, and he knew he could get a conversation going.

"I dunno. I've just had it, Mr. Williamson. Just feels like everything's squeezing in all around me."

"Well, tell me what's going on. This is John, my mentor. He's a coach, but instead of coaching a ball team or an academic team, he works with principals. We're going to listen and let you just get it all out."

The young boy wiped his eyes and sat back in the couch Brad kept in his office.

"Mainly, Mr. Williamson, I can't do it anymore. Mom and Dad are great parents, and I love them so, so much. But they want me to play every sport I played when I was little. That, plus the pressure here at school to be in everything coming and going, and I'm basically working twelve-hour days, sometimes more if I count homework. My Saturdays are filled up with some type of practice or competition all the time, too. There's never a break, not even in the summer. I used to love school, but lately, I just feel like a knot inside all the time."

"Bill, it sounds to me like we're all expecting you to be Super Kid because that's what you've always done from the time you were a first grader. Have you discussed your overload and how you're feeling with your parents?"

"I've tried to, but it just seems to hurt them. I can't get out what I'm really trying to say, and later, I feel guilty for even trying to explain."

"Would it help if Mrs. Thompson here made an appointment with your mom and dad and shared with them what you just shared with me?"

"I guess so."

"And what can I do to help take some of the pressure off here at school?"

"Well, I need to not be so involved in everything. Even cutting back on a couple of clubs would help. I just need some time, Mr. Williamson, to be a kid again."

When Millie and Billy left the room, Brad didn't know what to say. For the longest time, both he and John just sat and stared at the floor.

John spoke first. "I wonder how many others?"

"What, John?"

"How many other kids are good students, gifted in so many different areas, and because of that, we just push them and push them until at some point they snap. I remember a conversation with one of my boys. The summer before his senior year, he and I were discussing college. I said something like, 'Well, son, you could always go to a small school and play baseball. Your mother and I would love to watch you play on the college level these next four years.' He just looked at me and said, 'Dad, I've played baseball from the time I was six years old, every spring and summer since T-ball days. After this senior season, I'm done. I may never pick up a ball glove again in my life.'"

"What did you say, John?"

"I just stared for a minute, and then I said, 'Has it been that painful?' He looked me square in the eye and said, 'For a couple of years now, Dad, it's been more like a job than a hobby or the sport I used to love. But I knew it meant a lot to you and Mom for me to keep playing.'"

"What did you say then?"

"I just hugged him and told him how proud I was of him, and I hoped I had never put pressure on him to pursue his interests and talents for the wrong reasons. He smiled and said, 'You haven't, Dad. I'm glad I've played ball all these years. I don't regret it. But I can tell you, I have friends who have not kept the balance I have because their folks and others just pushed and pushed them to do more. They're seventeen and eighteen years old and already burned out. A couple of them are hinting that they're so tired of the demands that surround school, they may not go to college.'"

John's voice broke. "It was on that day, Brad, that I had to take a long, hard look at the priorities we adults have, and whether they align well with what our students need at the various stages of their development."

"Do you think Bill is one of those who's been pushed so hard that he's already burning out?"

"Yes, Brad, I think Bill is the classic case of the kid who is leaned on by everyone to perform. What does that say about what the adults in his life value most in him? Do we look deep into his soul and see a bright young man who has so many gifts he will have an entire life to sort them all out and use them at the appropriate times? Or do we see him as a commodity?"

"A commodity?"

"Something that we need to use as much as we can while there's still time—before he moves on to another grade, another school."

"That makes my knees weak, John. I understand your question. I wonder, too, how many others there are. What can we do about this?"

"I wonder if we could discuss this in the staff discussions I am facilitating about emotional intelligence and effective teams. Maybe we should also go a step further and dive into this whole question of overworking the high achievers. Think about it, Brad. Bill is working twelve- and fifteen-hour days to keep up with his studies and extracurricular responsibilities. That's a work-load that's more than his parents, or you, or I keep up with. Abundant living is not about producing at all costs. It's about balance—one of the secrets for living a fulfilling life."

John paused for a moment. "Maybe we should build this into Millie's advisor-advisee project, too. The kids need to be helped with this critical piece of life management. It's not just time management; it's the day-to-day priorities that make all the difference between those who have a healthy handle on life and those who don't."

"What about the other end of the spectrum, John?"

"What do you mean?"

"What about the kids who underachieve? We have students in all three of our centers who are either lazy or don't know how to stay focused on their schoolwork. Having the free Mondays for homework and projects has helped, but we still have some coasters who wreak havoc on what our teachers are trying to do in the classroom day after day. And these same kids will often not get involved in extracurricular activities."

John shook his head from side to side. "They don't get it. They don't understand that this is their ticket to a wonderful and fulfilling life."

"Yes! For example, John, we have one boy who is amazing to watch in PE class. He's one of the best natural athletes I've ever seen for his age, and he could no doubt play soccer in college if he'd apply himself while he's in high school. He wants to play on our team, but he says he doesn't want to practice every day the rest of the team practices. He says it will mess up his evening schedule."

"What is his evening schedule?"

"He loafs with a group of older kids, and to be honest, often they're up to no good."

"Well, Brad, we've touched on both ends of the spectrum. They're just kids, and I think your new advisor-advisee program, plus honest discussions with your staff, can head you in the direction of helping students make smarter choices as they move through their school careers. The habits they form at this young age stay with them their entire lives."

"But there's one key group we've left out, John."

"What group is that?"

"Parents."

"You're right. What do you suggest?"

"I think, as we lay this issue on the table with our staff and our kids, we need to develop a system of one-to-one student interviews with every middle schooler and high schooler we have in the Smith School project. Then, from those notes, we need to share this student feedback in one-to-one conferences with every parent we serve. With our counselors helping and Millie and I coordinating, we could pull this off between now and the start of second semester."

"Then I agree, Brad—you should do it as soon as you can and not put it off as something you might get to later."

"But after these three strands of addressing the issue—talking to the students about this in advisor-advisee, devoting staff meeting time to the topic, and then having one-to-one parent conferences to share our findings and get their input—then what?"

"Brad, from there, you could easily go to a true, authentic individual education plan for every kid in this school that included their extracurricular interests, hobbies, and so on. Then, every quarter, the parents would meet with a member of your staff and discuss in detail how the plan is going and what adjustments need to be made. The plan would hold everyone accountable—the student, the staff, the parents. A child would never fall though the cracks or work themselves to a point of physical and emotional exhaustion, as we witnessed with Bill today."

"An ongoing plan that we monitor all the time, with the student's input, our input, and the parents right in the middle of the plan from middle school to the night their child graduates."

"Exactly. And Brad, with the small school you have here, this is very, very doable."

"Well, this is the year the superintendent said he wants us to reinvent everything we have done that is not working well. I don't want any more Billys, John. And I don't want any more dropouts, or kids lollygagging their way through and us sitting back as if we're helpless. I'm in. But let's don't give it one of our typical school titles."

Brad doodled with his pen for a minute or so, then a big smile came to his face. "Let's call it 'Student Training in Effective Priority Systems'— STEPS."

"I like it Brad. This has success written all over it."

"Success for the kids, John . . . no, not just success—life fulfillment. That's what we should be about—every student equipped for a life of fulfillment. To often, the old model pushed kids through school, and then left them on their own to survive the best they could. For so many, it hasn't worked very well."

In *The Truth About Burnout*, Christina Maslach and Michael P. Leiter (1997) address the alarming prevalence of burnout in organizations across our culture. As educators, we must ask ourselves when does this condition begin, and what role do we play in abetting high achievers to develop this tendency?

Summary

When one of Smith School's top students breaks down in Brad's office due to overload and burnout, Brad and John discuss a better system that would include students, teachers, and parents working together to develop and monitor individual student learning plans all the way through middle and high school.

Reflection:

1. Do you have students who seem to be 'super kids,' involved in everything the school has to offer, but also at times seeming exhausted and already tired of school?
2. What does your school do with the underachievers? Is there an intervention philosophy that says, "We will not let you slide through school"?
3. Are parents included in the development of customized semester or yearly plans for each student in your school?

CHAPTER ELEVEN

~

Leadership Team

The king used to make all the decisions, and the kingdom struggled—
until his advisors showed him a better way.

The Monday morning of Thanksgiving week, John called and asked Brad
if he wanted to help him find a Christmas tree on his granddad's old farm
that evening. Brad was trying to catch up on everything he could before the
holiday started, but knew he needed to get away from the grind, so he agreed.
As they drove in John's pickup toward the old home place, he could tell Brad
had something serious on his mind.

"Son, you're awfully deep in thought. What are you cooking up now? I'd say
you've had a pretty good fall semester—want to give it a rest for a few days?"

Brad grinned and chuckled under his breath. "No, I've just been thinking
about the reality check we had with Billy the other day. That last phrase we
discussed, 'every student equipped for a life of fulfillment,' I wrote that down,
and it captures my vision of what every school should be. I shared it with our
teachers in our faculty meeting this week, and everyone liked it. But how do
I make it come to life? How do I make it something that we're passionate
about at Smith School?"

"It does have an effective ring to it, Brad. Stirs something deep inside. Let
me ask you, how is your advisory council going at school?"

"Since the fire, we've been so busy getting back on our feet, we've only
met once all fall. And that's my fault. But we normally meet at least quarterly, so I do have our winter session planned for next week."

"Well, I suggest that you put this item on the agenda and get some feedback from the group."

"That's just it, John. We get so bogged down in the business of school that I think sometimes we forget that we are the leadership team for the school. And I take full responsibility for the lack of focus. I have good intentions, but every time we meet it seems by the time I run through the agenda of items we have to discuss formally, our time is up and we've basically rubber stamped a lot of paperwork."

"What if you took all that information that takes up so much time and gave each member of your council a folder that they could look through later, and then for this upcoming meeting, have only one item on the agenda?"

"One item? What would it be?"

"Vision."

"Vision?"

"Yep. Then, under that heading, list in this order: core values, mission, strategy, structure, and future."

"Now you've really lost me, John. What kind of an agenda is that?"

"It's an agenda that, if followed every month, would take your school council from the 'dotting the i, crossing the t' club to a true leadership team that's excited about its meetings because those meetings are going to be about transforming Smith School, not just business as usual."

"So, vision as the main item?"

"Yes, and for starters, throw your phrase out there to be discussed. How does it go again?"

"'Every student equipped for a life of fulfillment.' But as I think about it more, I want to add 'and service' at the end of it. So, how does 'every student equipped for a life of fulfillment and service' sound?"

"I like it a lot. What a powerful statement. After your leadership team has settled on this, or something similar, I'd put it on letterheads, on e-mail salutations, on school newsletters. Even on a big banner in the front lobby and in other parts of the building, too."

"So everyone will know that's what we really want to be about, and more and more students, staff, and parents will start internalizing it."

"Exactly."

"But John, next on your list was core values. How does that fit?"

"Because they are the nonnegotiables that should drive everything about Smith School. And you've been working on these this fall already, it seems to me."

"What do you mean?"

"What have you been doing in regard to reading and math?"

"Making them true core values—so every child at Smith School can read well and do math well."

"And your new advisor-advisee program? Same thing."

"Now I'm starting to get it, John. We put on the agenda first that which we value the most, and have rich discussions about our menu of services and what could be made better. Keep going. You've got my attention, old man . . . Sorry. I mean, wise mentor."

Both men had a good laugh, and John went on. "Mission. What is the school's mission, Brad?"

"To realize the vision. In reality, that's why we're even here, John, as the staff of Smith School, to inspire these kids to learn and learn well—so they're prepared for life and passionate about life. What's next on your list?"

"Strategy."

"Here's where we talk about the nuts and bolts of what's working and what's not, right?"

"You're getting it, Brad. In every council meeting, or maybe 'leadership team' is a more appropriate description, when you get to this part, jot down notes and assign tasks to staff and parent teams. You'll also want to survey students for their input from time to time."

"John, it actually sounds like fun. Is it possible that business meetings can be fun?"

"Oh, but they're not just business meetings, Brad. They're vision meetings."

"You're right. If they're boring and the same old routine every time we meet, we've missed the point, haven't we? Now what follows strategy, John?"

"Structure. This is crucial, Brad, and we often miss it in how we run our schools. Basically, this is your master schedule, the flow of the school day, how you prioritize everyone's time in the school—from custodian, to student, to teacher, to your secretary, to you, and everyone in between."

"So, if we have disruptions that are detracting from instructional time, such as scheduling an assembly at a terrible time of the week or using the intercom during class periods, these are examples of poor structure."

"Well said, Brad. Much of the downfall of schools that are, to put it bluntly, mediocre, is in how they don't do structure well. But healthy structure is not just the flow of the schedule and everyone being where they are supposed to at all times of the day. It's also the flow inside the classroom. So, a school that is instructionally structured well will have a staff that is always honing its skills on the finer points of good teaching."

"And that takes all of us, starting with me and my life skills class—reading, and training, and visiting other schools—always working on getting better as mentors of our students. And let's see, there was one more. What was it?"

"Future."

"Future! Yes, I love that one, John. I'm assuming at this final stage of the meeting we set goals and timelines, assign tasks, things like that."

"That's part of it, Brad, but not all of it. Future is indeed about short-term and long-term goals. It's a living, breathing, working draft strategic plan, if you will, but its most important role is the freedom this part of the meeting should allow for seeing what the future of Smith School can be. Once your leadership team, and any others who will, start dreaming about what could be, that 'could be' will eventually become reality. It's a powerful concept, and it works."

"Wow, John, with this approach, I'll have people knocking themselves down to be on this leadership team."

"Good! That's what you want. And don't leave them out, Brad. Create 'think tank' teams that help do the work, invite everyone to these sessions, encourage ideas and suggestions from all stakeholders at the school and in the community. Empower and equip, and your school will never look back."

"Empower and equip?"

"Yes, give people the training and the tools they need, then set them free. Look around you at the array of talent on your staff and in your students, your parents and other volunteers, plus the other resources from the Smithtown community, and turn them loose to make this school all it can be. It's a city on a hill, not a stoic institution. It's alive. It's one of the grandest adventures that anyone could be a part of. A school community is an oasis and a bridge to endless possibility all rolled into one, if only we will let it be."

"This is giving me goosebumps, John."

"Good! We need more educators with goosebumps, Brad. That means you're excited about your work. It makes all the difference. . . . Hey, we're here. I brought an extra pair of gloves for you. Let's go find us a Christmas tree!"

In *Nine Lessons of Successful School Leadership Teams*, Bill McKeever and the California School Leadership Academy (2003) offer key principles for utilizing the collective talents of a team of leaders in creating an innovative, student-centered school.

Summary

Brad shares with John that his school council meetings get bogged down with trivial items that don't allow time for real discussion of the school's vision and how to bring it to reality. John explains the concept of a leadership team and shares a formula that would help Brad's leadership meetings take on an inspiring flavor.

Reflection:

1. What is your school's vision? How are you getting there?
2. How does your school's leadership team avoid getting bogged down with minutiae during its meetings?
3. What are the three most important goals your school has for better meeting the needs of its students? Are you making steady progress?

CHAPTER TWELVE

~

The Road That Leads Home

> The journey is long and hard, and the wise traveler discerns in advance
> what must go with him and what can be left behind.

As December came with all of its magic, John couldn't believe that the first semester was coming to a close. He and Liz took Brad and Angie out to a dinner and holiday show to celebrate the season, and afterward, they invited the young couple over to their house for some evening relaxation. John and Liz's kids were home, and they helped make the Williamsons feel welcome. As the ladies took a tour of the house, John and Brad settled in for a late-night chat in the den.

"Thank you, John, for inviting us to join you this evening. Angie and I have been so impressed with you and your family. What's your secret?"

"To be honest, Brad, it's the same principle that we were discussing the other day on our way to get the tree. It's about priorities. When I was just starting out as a principal, many years ago, I didn't understand 'first things first.' And, soon, I was drowning, not only as a school leader, but also here at home. Fortunately, I started figuring it out."

"What came first in your transformation?"

"I began to realize that my job was overwhelming, and it always would be if I didn't make some personal changes. So, I let go of the Superman, 'always be in control' mentality, and started getting to know my staff and students on a one-to-one relationship level. As a result, I slowed down. I became very focused on what it means to be a servant leader, and from that point, I soon found myself very fulfilled in my work. Once I started putting my people first, everything changed."

"Could Liz tell a difference?"

"Oh sure, and so could our kids. I was home earlier from school, instead of later. I started exercising, eating healthy, sleeping right. And I got my spiritual life in order. Pretty soon, I felt half my age, and Liz told me that now she couldn't wait for me to get home in the evenings, because she knew who was going to walk through that door."

"I bet your staff could tell a difference, too."

"Oh my, yes. It was like night and day. I was no longer swimming upstream, so they could relax and not have to also try to swim upstream to keep up with me. We started talking about our school's priorities in our staff meetings, and what should come first. Obviously, it was the kids. So, day by day, month by month, year by year, we kept improving our delivery model, our total package of how we met the holistic needs of the students who attended our school."

John smiled and went on. "Self-leadership is contagious, Brad. Of course, as we matured as a staff, that meant our relationships with parents went to a higher level, too. After a while, the community started to notice, other schools started to notice. Heritage Elementary was known as a school that celebrated learning—an authentic community where everyone knew your name and where you could be creative, explore, and grow."

"John, I have trouble sometimes being patient with a couple of my teachers. They may not mean to, but they come across as being very self-serving and not committed to our Smith School project. How do I bring them along without treating them as my black sheep, my immature staff who drain the life right out of the rest of us?"

"I know, Brad, I know. It seems every principal has a couple of staff members who seem to have chosen the wrong profession, and they are determined to make everyone else in the building pay for it. But, in reality, these are not folks to be thrown on the junk heap. Instead, they are reclamation projects, and so critical to the culture of your school becoming healthy and something all of you can be proud of."

"So what do I do?"

"Pay attention to them. Listen to their suggestions and their complaints. Often, they are right when they see a flaw in the process. Put them on a team where their strengths will contribute, maybe even make them the chair of a project. Stop in to chat often, get to know the names of their children, their hobbies, where they went to school."

Brad could feel John's passion for relating to people, and realized that this was John's secret—a strength that could be measured in how it positively impacted other lives.

"You mentor by caring first, Brad. Then later mentor by matching them with a master teacher who will also put relationship first. Send them to observe at other schools, help them develop a very detailed and helpful growth plan, and sit down and discuss it often. Make sure to compliment what they are doing well—don't just point out weaknesses. If they are serious about teaching, you'll see them start coming around. If they're not, they'll usually leave politely. Either way, your respect for them and genuine caring as their supervisor will have a lasting impression on them and on your other staff, too."

"Wow! That must take lots of getting your own ego and feelings out of the way, John!"

"It does. But that's the whole point, Brad. You see, as the principal, you're the shepherd. There's a big difference between being a shepherd and being a boss. This whole concept of teaching and learning is about the mentor and the pupil, and that includes the adult relationships in the school community. Once I learned to see my role as the helper and supporter of my staff, not the overassertive supervisor who maintained order no matter who got their feelings hurt, I never got mad at a staff person again."

"Never?"

"Oh, don't get me wrong. I was disappointed a couple of times, but never mad. Like me, they were human. Like me, they were going to make mistakes. Like me, they needed support and someone to believe in them."

"Is this the approach you took toward parents, too?"

"Sure did. And with parents, as with my staff, I realized they mainly just needed someone to listen while they shared their perspectives. Actually, I learned more about the true culture and some of the weaknesses of our school by listening to my parents than I did from any other source of data I had. Think about it. Why would parents make an appointment to talk with the principal unless they or their children have experienced something that you need to hear about, something that you probably will not hear about otherwise—at least not their side of the story."

"Makes sense, John."

"And Brad, parents are such allies of the school. They want their kids to do well, to learn. This is where that emotional intelligence that we've been helping your staff with comes in. Parents are eager to have respectful, trusting, two-way relationships with teachers and administrators. But we've got to meet them on turf where they feel comfortable, not just in a heated meeting in the principal's office after a bad grade or an incident at school. We need to be building healthy relationships earlier, not later."

"How did you see your role with the students, John?"

"At first, I felt like I needed to come across as the general. After a while, I realized the kids didn't need that type of a role model nearly as much as they needed a leader they could respect and feel close to. So I made myself get out of the office and away from all that endless paperwork, and I walked around the school campus several times a day. I dropped in on classes and just hung out for a while. I'd sit with kids at lunch. I'd go on field trips. I'd add humor on my intercom announcements and in assemblies when I could. I'd go to ball games and other after-school activities regularly. I got my 'boss man' ego out of the way and lightened up.

"Brad, the school culture should not be so rigid that we all put on a different face when we walk into the building. An effective school is a community of people working and growing together every day. I think sometimes we make this whole arena of school way too serious. And in so doing, the staff, the kids, volunteers, visitors—they're all wondering how to get out as fast as they can. And the kids, too often, are so bored it's embarrassing."

"So how did you deal with that dilemma?"

"I started making time to sit down with each teacher every quarter to work on their individual growth plan. One thing they knew I expected to see in their daily teaching habits was a variety of activities that made school more engaging for their students. From technology to learning centers, from guest speakers to field trips, from plays to theme days . . . as a staff, we learned to enjoy our teaching. And the kids learned as they had never learned before."

"Learning and enjoyment. What a novel concept!"

Both men chuckled and shook their heads, as if to say, "Parts of the system have been so broken, if it weren't so funny, we'd cry."

In *The Four Dimensions of Principal Leadership*, Reginald Leon Green (2009) builds a comprehensive framework for leading twenty-first-century schools that includes self-leadership, relationship building, organizational life, and other key leadership practices that can transform schools.

Summary

John shares with Brad his formula for being an authentic, effective leader, which he learned early in his career as he spiraled downward at school and at home. When John realized that his work was about relationships and service, he changed from being a boss to being someone who cared, and thus someone who made a difference.

Reflection:

1. Is the pace at school so grueling that you have noticed the strain it puts on your principal?
2. Is your school relationship driven? If not, why not?
3. Are healthy relationships between staff, with students, and with parents fiercely protected at your school? Which comes first, relationships or getting work done at all costs?

CHAPTER THIRTEEN

~

Facing the Enemy

I ran as fast as I could to get away from that complicated, self-focused person who worked so hard to destroy me. It never worked. Finally, one day I realized—my enemy was me. And then the healing began.

John scheduled his next principals cohort session for the Monday after the schools in the region let out for Christmas break. This particular meeting was held at Blue Creek High School. Todd, Blue Creek's principal, whom John had mentored the previous year, met him at the door with a big grin on his face and a long hug.

"I'm so glad you called, John. I wanted to become involved in your group, and I'm honored to host this month's session. And you were right—it's been another great year. We've stayed focused on our core values, relationships, and people first, and on what our data tells us is working well and is not working well. And we're still doing those student surveys. What they tell us about our blind spots is always so right on target."

"Wonderful, Todd! I want you to share your success story with the rest of the group today, too."

As John opened the session with introductions and passed out some servant leadership resources he thought would be helpful, he could feel the air of relaxation and relief as these young school leaders relished the fact that they had wrapped up the first semester. But one man, who appeared to be in mid-career, was unimpressed with the principle of servant leadership that John emphasized in these sessions and in the e-mails he sent to the group regularly.

"I guess I just don't get it, John. This whole concept of servant leadership—it just doesn't work for me."

"How do you mean, Charles?"

"Well, come on, my students would laugh me out of the school if I came across this way. It seems more like 'Mr. Rogers' stuff. I don't mean to appear insulting, but aren't there other models that you would recommend for those of us who work at the tougher schools?"

"No, not really, Charles. Every leadership style has its merits, I guess, as long as it is based in integrity and ethics. But see, that's where I can't get away from the servant leadership approach. Its bottom line is the 'goodness' factor. How can you go wrong with that? It's the very fabric of human relationship—of how communities learn to coexist effectively."

"But don't students, and even teachers, take advantage of you when you overemphasize this model?"

"No. Quite the contrary. Once they understand it, they embrace it. Oh sure, at first, there will be a teacher or two who will try to take advantage, and some students will try to force you to not care for them. But that's the beauty of it; servant leadership is not about you and your feelings. It's about meeting the needs of others. So, you just work to find creative ways to meet the needs of the students and staff who tend to rebel and create unnecessary tension. And notice I said unnecessary tension."

As John stopped and took a drink of water from his glass, he noticed that not one person was moving. Their eyes were all fixed on him. He knew that this was a crucial teaching moment, and what he was explaining was different from what some in the group had been told in the past.

He continued, "Servant leadership is not about weakness and artificial harmony. It is just the opposite. It empowers and equips everyone in the organization to be free to explore, create, look for better answers, grow to a level they perhaps did not think was possible."

"Doesn't such a culture create chaos?"

"Sometimes, yes. And sometimes, for the organization to overcome its dysfunction, you need some chaos, Charles. This is a great discussion. Someone else in the group give me an example."

Millie held her hand up. "Well, when our school burned this summer, we definitely went through some pretty serious chaos. But, ironically, looking back, it opened the door for us to reinvent ourselves. Now, just a semester later, we are so much stronger as a school. We have gotten rid of the distractions that were keeping us from being an effective school that inspired our students. Now, we're driven by a relentless focus on community and the exciting learning going on every day in every classroom."

Charles seemed agitated. "But what about the loss of your campus? You guys don't even have a gym now. How can you say you're better? Aren't you divided up into three little buildings, without nearly the resources you used to have?"

Millie smiled. "Yes, we lost some physical resources. But what we have discovered in the process, how to really tap into our human resources, has been so much more crucial for the many needs of our students. Perhaps we were hiding behind the physical building, as if it were the school. We've had an epiphany. The school has very little to do with the physical plant. We, the human capital, are the school."

John was amazed at how well Millie had explained the transformation at Smith School, and he added, "Brad and Millie's school has experienced something that is very good for an organization. Literally, the walls of their building came down, releasing the staff, students, parents, and the entire community to start over with their vision of a boundaryless, unchained learning center. Yes, it is a very nonlinear model, but that's good. Sometimes, to make significant improvement, we need to get away from the tradition and the predictable structure that we've become attached to over the years."

"What do you mean by nonlinear?" Charles was no longer sarcastic, he seemed genuinely curious.

John went on, "Nonlinear is actually what helps society to improve. It's utilizing our divergent thinking skills and finding not just acceptable solutions, but the best solutions. For example, at my former school, a couple of years ago, the new principal implemented an intramural program that went far beyond the traditional team sports model that had existed there for years. She found a 'win, win' that allowed dozens more of her students to participate in team sports while in elementary school. She had the courage to go counterculture, a very nonlinear route, but one that the community embraced and one that made her school much more student centered."

Todd spoke up. "I can share an example from right here at Blue Creek High School. When John started mentoring me one on one I couldn't stand it. I didn't have time, and I resented someone coming in and daring to discuss with me the things that were not going well in our building. But John didn't force the servant leadership model on me. He helped build a trusting relationship with me first, then together we started tackling my personal leadership gaps one by one. For me, that was the whole issue. I myself had to start thinking more nonlinearly. I had become your classic 'good old boy,' politically correct, washed-up principal at the age of thirty-two."

"What did you do differently?" Charles was now taking notes.

Todd's voice cracked as he looked at John with tears in his eyes. "I got out of the way so my school could be free again. Now, mind you, I thought I was already out of the way. In fact, I had become so disconnected with everyone that I had my assistant principals doing teachers' meetings so I could avoid my staff. I dodged tough issues. I hated assemblies where I had to speak to the student body. I mainly hung out with my coaches and rooted for our ball teams. It was all about me and my comfort zone."

Todd grabbed a napkin and wiped tears from his face. "When I finally looked at myself in the mirror and admitted what a weak leader I had become, I got my pathetic ego out of the way. John helped me to focus on others, and gradually, I noticed that when I did that, everything changed. I was no longer a symbol of mediocrity and the 'game' of school. Instead, I started pitching in to help people work smarter so the school would be a good place to be, a learning center everyone in the community could be proud of. The kids, the staff, the parents—they all noticed. I was no longer in it for me. I was in it for them."

John smiled and looked at Charles. "And I might add that Todd took several volatile issues head-on last year, including confrontation with two abusive teachers who are no longer on his staff. He named his lead custodian the staff person of the year and worked her shift one evening. He brought his office staff and cafeteria staff up on stage at graduation and recognized them as servant leaders who helped carry the school. And I remember many other examples. But, suffice it to say, he was not a weak leader anymore. By learning to serve, he also learned courage. It was an honor to work with him."

In *Leading in a Culture of Change*, Michael Fullan (2001) advocates the need for caring relationships and moral purpose to be key parts of the equation in how school leaders transform schools.

Summary

During a principals cohort session, John is challenged by a member of the group who doesn't feel that servant leadership is always an effective model for school change. Several examples shared by other principals illustrate that John's model includes having the courage to challenge the status quo and to make bold changes when they eliminate careless practices.

Reflection:

1. How would you define the leadership style in your school?
2. Is conflict handled in a fair and healthy way in your school?
3. Does your school culture reflect an understanding of the concept of serving others?

CHAPTER FOURTEEN

~

The Peril of Delay is Costly

One by one, the pillars crumbled, as the palace guards would not believe that the foundation was old and in decay.

At the turn of the school year, when second semester begins, there is often a calm for several weeks as the colder weather makes the classroom a cozy place to be. So Brad was shocked when a letter arrived in early January that indicated someone was working behind the scenes to derail the Smith School project. He called John, and John came by that same morning.

"Take a look at this, John. Someone has written a scathing letter to the state department, unsigned, and made all kinds of accusations about what we're trying to do here this year."

John read the four-page letter, which claimed that the three-school model that the Smithtown district had adopted was a sham and demanded a thorough investigation.

"I'm surprised the state even sent it to you unsigned, Brad."

"They wouldn't have, but our superintendent has a good friend there who thought we deserved a heads-up. He told the superintendent that the state was ignoring it, since they had no proof of anything other than good, creative teaching and learning going on that other schools could learn from."

"I don't see any negative evidence in the letter, either, Brad. Mainly, the person who wrote this feels the traditional system of schooling was doing just fine and is insulted that your model here would take such a divergent route. Son, remember, when you implement change, it takes some folks a while to accept it."

"Even if they can see that it's working better than the old model?"

"Yep."

"Are we really making a difference, John? Reading something like this really takes the wind out of my sails."

"Yes, you are definitely making a difference, Brad, by blazing these new trails, and here's why. We forget sometimes to step back and see the long view. The reality is painful. Here's the fast version of a speech I was asked to give a few weeks ago to a group of principals down state who wanted to know more about the schools I have been mentoring and how they have addressed the gaps—the parts of the system that are broken. I'll try not to get to preaching too much here. But did you know?"

And John recalled from his speech, "The U.S. government has admitted that it projects how many prisons it will need in the future by looking at third-grade reading data. Across the U.S., some estimates have it that around thirty percent of ninth graders do not make it to their senior year to graduate with their class. They drop out. In some states, several counties have even more shocking numbers. Of those who do graduate from high school, only about a quarter will actually attain a college degree. In some states, it's more like twenty percent."

"I didn't realize it was that bad, John."

"Oh, there's more, Brad. I'm just getting started. Recent interviews of graduated high school students have revealed that they were bored in school, and they have many suggestions for how school could have been made more relevant for them, including more counselors, more challenging courses, more options in course selection, and so on. And colleges and universities are concerned that too many freshmen drop out of college, or struggle, in their first year. Many of these were A and B students in high school.

"Plus, Brad, with the explosion of Internet learning, schools are no longer a necessity for anyone, at any age. Mediocrity is no longer an option. We are not a monopoly anymore. Many students who go to summer camp don't want to come home. But many students who go back to school in the fall beg to stay home. Why is that?"

John's voice rose as he continued. "Many elementary teachers share that they are very frustrated with parents when they inherit first graders who can't read. Many middle school teachers share that they are very frustrated when they inherit adolescents who still can't read. Many high school teachers share that they are frustrated when they inherit fifteen- and sixteen-year-olds who still can't read.

"Yes, Brad, we have a problem. Not every kid comes from a teacher's home or is motivated by the traditional methods of schooling. But we continue on the same track we've used for decades and ask our teachers to do the impossible, hoping that when our 'customers' are nineteen, they'll get it. When they're nineteen, too often, they will need the rest of society to take care of them.

"And as we see with our current economic crisis, Brad, what some experts have been warning for years was on the way is now here. The formula we've used in the past will not sustain the American culture over the long haul. No, certainly, education is not solely to blame. We have done so many things well, actually. Where would our society be without the hard work of teachers and schools down through the decades? But parts of our system are certainly broken.

How do we fix it, John?"

John pointed his finger at Brad and looked square into his eyes with a fire that originated from deep within. "Politicians will not. How would they know how to anyway? It will be fixed by one wise and caring teacher at a time, one servant-leader principal at a time, one innovative school at a time. It will take years, but perhaps it's not too late."

"John, you're not talking about physical plants, complex systems, and playing it safe so when May rolls around we all can look back and say 'well done,' attaching 'well done' to whatever measures we want to attach it to, are you?"

"No, I'm not. I'm talking about authentic, one-to-one mentor and pupil models, however that can work best in each community. It may mean going back to the drawing board, like your school was forced to do. For way too long, we've looked at education through the lens of adults. We have built these massive organized structures that fit the needs of adults more than the needs of students. That's got to change."

In *The Index of Leading Cultural Indicators: American Society at the End of the Twentieth Century*, William J. Bennett (1999) offers alarming data that indicates that the American culture is experiencing a serious meltdown of the core values formerly looked upon as the guiding principles of this country.

Summary

Brad is discouraged when he finds out that his new school project has been challenged by an anonymous letter to the state department, but John shares with him why bold, nonlinear schooling models like the Smithtown project must be pursued. John's examples of glaring gaps in the effectiveness of the traditional educational system are sobering.

Reflections:

1. How do we address interviews with former high school students that indicate they were bored in school?
2. Does your school conduct exit interviews with students as they graduate from various grade levels?
3. What variables impact your school's ability to reinvent as needed? How can these factors be addressed?

CHAPTER FIFTEEN

∼

Loss of a Friend

To know and to be blessed by a person of goodness is a treasure that cannot be measured.

Millie called Brad in the middle of the night, sobbing with the news. Mrs. Crabtree had passed away at the hospital after suffering a heart attack the evening before. She had taught second grade at Smith School for thirty-three years, and was loved by all who knew her. John had been on the road working with another school, but he stopped by Smithtown that evening on his way home. Brad was at the elementary center with Millie, still consoling staff, students, and others who were dropping by to mourn and to pay tribute to one of the community's matriarchs.

"John, it's such a blow to Smithtown, such a blow. Practically everyone in this county knew Mrs. Crabtree, and most of us had her in school. She was one of my all-time favorite teachers, and I still have some of the work I did in her class at home in a scrapbook. I can just hear her pushing me to be the best that I could be: 'Now, Bradley, is that your best work? If it is, fine. If you're rushing, let's spend some more time on it. You're going to be a fine, upstanding man when you grow up someday, and you'll never be happy unless you do your best work.'"

"Pretty powerful lesson, wasn't it, son?"

"Oh my yes, John, and she was always doing that. Mrs. Crabtree taught this town more about character when we were seven-year-olds than all the books we read put together. It was in everything she did at school, and away from school, too. How can I capture all of that in one five-minute talk?"

"What do you mean?"

"Her family has asked me to represent the school and say a few words at the funeral. I'm at a loss over how to do her justice. How do you pay last respects properly in just a few words?"

"Would the family give you more time?"

"How's that?"

"What if not just one, but several of her former students told their favorite stories, stories that capture what a wonderful person and mentor she was. Perhaps add photographs and video clips of her life as a teacher down through the years and celebrate her contribution to education in a way that would make her proud."

Brad replied immediately, "I think that's exactly what I'll do."

Mrs. Crabtree's funeral was held in the largest church in town, which was ironically the school center she had been teaching at this year, and the line at visitation the night before stretched down the sidewalk for three blocks. Smithtown cancelled school for her funeral, and Brad explained in a beautiful, poetic way what John had been helping him to understand in their discussions all year—that teaching is about relationships and the varying, unique needs of each student. Then, an older, skinny, bearded man in a flannel shirt and blue jeans followed Brad to the pulpit.

"I reckon I'd have never made it through school if not for Mrs. Crabtree. I got behind when I started, and I stayed behind that second year until around Thanksgiving. Then one day, she said, 'Simon, that's it boy. This is the last day of you and me dodging the obvious. It's time you learned to read. Meet me right here after school at my desk. We'll stay one hour every day until Christmas, take a two-week break, and then do the same thing until Easter.' And, by George, that's exactly what we did. By the time I was finished with second grade, I could read right up there with Tommy, Sallie, Mary, and all the others."

Simon looked surprised when the audience clapped for him in a spontaneous ovation. "I went on to work down at the local wholesale store, and if I hadn't been able to read, I'd have never landed that job. Still work there today. I raised a family and now I'm helping raise my grandkids thanks to that store. But really, it was Mrs. Crabtree who turned me around, because I was already thinking about the day I could quit school when she took me under her wing."

A woman followed Simon to the pulpit. "Hello. I'm the Sallie that Simon just mentioned. I have a different type of story to tell. Actually, I always did well in school. It came easy for me. But I made a mistake when I was seventeen, and the next thing I knew, I was with child. I was so humiliated, I quit school the fall of my senior year. One day, lo and behold, who should show up on my parents' doorstep but Mrs. Crabtree. She had heard about my struggles, and she came by to have a talk."

Sallie stopped for a moment to regain her composure—sniffles could be heard all around the sanctuary. "You all know how she loved to chat with her former students whenever she'd run into us around town. Well, on that morning, on the couch in the living room, we did more crying than talking. But when she left, I promised her I'd go back to school the following week. And I did. How blessed I have been that she took the time to help me see that one mistake does not have to ruin your whole life. And today, that little baby, my Suzanne, is a teacher herself. I remind her often of how much her students need her to love them the way Mrs. Crabtree loved all of us."

More men and women followed Sallie, each with a story to tell about Mrs. Crabtree:

"I'm Junior Savage, your sheriff. Something some of you don't know is that there was a time back in high school when I just about ruined my life with alcohol. One Saturday morning, I was sitting in jail, crying, after another night of drinking and making a fool of myself. In walks Mrs. Crabtree, and she says, 'Junior, no more. You were the smartest kid in my class, and here you are throwing your life away on booze. Are you man enough to pick yourself up by the bootstraps and enroll in college if I'd pay your first semester for you?'

"I said, 'Yes, ma'am, I think I am.' She said, 'You better be. What do you want to be, Junior?' 'I'd love to study law enforcement, Mrs. Crabtree.' 'Okay,' she said, 'one semester. That's all I'll pay for. And if you ever drink again, you owe me the money back for that semester. You're a borderline alcoholic, son, so it's cold turkey from now on. Deal?' With tears in my eyes, I said, 'Deal,' and I started a new life."

"I'm Margie Leadingham. I'm an accountant, so I work with numbers for a living. There was never anyone, in all my years of school, who could make math come alive like it did in Mrs. Crabtree's room. Before my year with her, I sort of liked it. After that year, I loved it."

"I'm Pete Swanson. My oldest boy, Nate, was killed in a car wreck three weeks before his high school graduation fifteen years ago. All of you took such good care of us during that nightmare, and I'm eternally grateful. But Mrs. Crabtree came over and visited with me on our front porch about once a month for a year after the accident. She always had such great stories to tell of how Nate excelled in her room as the class comedian. Others saw that as a liability, but she saw it as a special gift. Nate would always tell me how Mrs. Crabtree made him feel big because she loved his humor and laughed at his jokes."

One by one, for about forty-five minutes, the tributes were shared. One lady remembered Mrs. Crabtree giving her a kitten when she thought she was getting nothing for Christmas the year she was seven. Another man said she'd made sure he had a job the summer before he started mechanics school, when he had almost decided not to go to school because of the cost. He mowed her yard and trimmed her shrubbery well into the fall, and she paid him twice what the other lawnkeepers were making in town at that time.

At last, Mrs. Crabtree's oldest daughter stood, with eyes full of tears, and said, "Plain and simple, teaching was her life. It was her passion, her calling, . . . her best chance to make a contribution to humanity. And she took it and ran with it. I used to be jealous, because she seemed to love it so. But as I got older, I realized, what an honor to be raised and loved by someone so gifted with such compassion for others."

Then, one last person came forward. "They told me I'm supposed to close this part of the service. I'm Cynthia Edwards. I don't live here anymore. I went away to college, majored in political science, and believe it or not, I am a state representative. I remember vividly how Mrs. Crabtree somehow found time to make history and government and current events come alive. I would come home talking about these grown-up things and my dad would just die laughing. But guess what? Something stirred in me even way back then. I want to read you a letter that Mrs. Crabtree sent me in the mail just a few months ago. I'm told she sent dozens of these to former students year after year.

Dear Cynthia,
My oh my, child, I am so proud of you! I read about your good work in the paper often, and save the clippings so I can give them to your mother at church. You can imagine how proud your folks and family are of you.

But I must tell you, Cynthia, I am not surprised at all that you have achieved what you have. I could tell the first day you walked into my second-grade room that you were going to conquer the world. You had that gleam in your eye, and you loved life and all the special things that come with it. I used to tell my fellow teachers that you helped make a party wherever you went. That's how much charisma and personality you had, even as a young child.

But, Cynthia, none of that would have gotten you very far if you hadn't had that goodness in your heart. It was touching to me to watch you treat your classmates so kindly and become one of our model students that now all of Smithtown is so, so in awe of. May all of your dreams keep coming true. And when you're in town next time, drop by to see me. I'll make us some tea, and we'll sit on the front porch and catch up on all that you're doing there in the capitol.

Love you, 'little girl,'
Mrs. Crabtree (Minnie)

Cynthia was the last speaker. After a song, the pastor closed the service with prayer, and John followed at the back of the procession to the cemetery. The line of cars stretched all the way through Smithtown.

As John drove, he thought, "How could one life touch so many? One loving teacher, one classroom. Oh, why haven't we figured this out? This is the answer." And he joined the many others that day who honored a great woman with tears rolling down their faces, as they realized a treasure had gone home.

In *To Know As We Are Known*, Parker J. Palmer (1993) speaks to the less-discussed reality that education is a spiritual journey. Teaching is so much more than assignments, projects, and data that measures success. Teaching is a heart-to-heart relationship.

Summary

One of Brad's veteran teachers, a legend in the community, passes away. At her funeral, the impact she has had on so many lives is revealed through testimonials offered by former students. John is reminded that this level of one-to-one connection and service through caring relationships is the very essence of the mentor-pupil model that we call school.

Reflection:

1. Who in your school has extended their teaching and caring for students into the community, far beyond the classroom?
2. How does your school celebrate and honor the matriarchs and patriarchs of your community?
3. In what ways does your school contribute to the life and health of the larger community? If it is having minimal impact, what changes need to be made to allow it to reach out further beyond its walls?

CHAPTER SIXTEEN

~

The Writer

It was there all along, trapped inside. All she needed was someone to take the time to notice. Soon, her passion broke free, and she breathed, and laughed, and loved, the genius inside now a blessing to the world.

A winter snow blanketed the region, and Smith School was out for the week, so John and Brad decided to spend some time together while the pace was slowed for a few days. A snowy hike in the woods away from the routine of work was just the change they needed, and Brad felt renewed as they drove back toward town.

"I've never had a better year, John. It just seems that everything runs more simply. I had no idea we could let go of the master schedule, and other pieces of our school operation that took years to build, and come out of the fray with something better. But we have."

"Yes, it's quite an amazing story, Brad. Smith School just may be the talk of the state soon. I'm getting more and more inquiries from other schools wanting to visit. They like what they hear about your simplified structure, the stress-free culture, and the focus on relationship-driven learning in every classroom."

"The mentor and the pupil, John, just like you explained early in the year. That's what we talk about in our staff and team meetings, in open houses, at PTA functions, in parent-teacher conferences."

"And I bet your teachers love it, now that they see how much less hectic a school day can be."

"Yes, and the kids love it, too. Let me share an example with you. Just last week, a student that I had a lot of trouble with last year, Harold Simmons, won a writing award at a regional literature and arts showcase. We're all so proud of him. But the key was the connection we made this year with him on the one-to-one level. Early in the year, his sophomore English teacher came by to see me, obviously frustrated.

"'I want him expelled as soon as possible, Mr. Williamson,' she barked as soon as she shut my office door. Her tone shocked me, John. I said something like, 'Whoa, slow down, Mrs. Cantrell. After you tell me what's happened, let's call the student in and see if there's not another solution.'"

"What happened next?" John leaned in closer as he shifted in his seat. This story intrigued him.

"Well, a few minutes later, we sent for Harold, and in walks this shy kid with a toothpick in the corner of his mouth and a ball cap on. I stayed calm, and in a low, quiet tone I asked, 'Harold, why won't you take off your ball cap for Mrs. Cantrell? You know our rules on wearing hats in class.'

"'Just don't want to, that's all.'

"I could see by her body language that Mrs. Cantrell was getting hot, so I said, 'Well, it's time to take it off or I'm going to have to call your dad and send you home.'

"At that instant, he burst into tears, John, and literally begged, 'No, Mr. Williamson. Please. Don't call Daddy.'

"I asked, 'Why, Harold?'

"'Because Daddy's who cut my hair, just as a drunken prank. He's also who bruised my back, and who ran Momma off. She's been gone for three days.'

"John, this kid was being abused on a daily basis, and once we got him some help and started working with him one-to-one every day here at school, it was like night and day."

"What did you do?"

"For starters, we got social services involved. They found the mother and immediately got her and her children out of the home. They are staying with her parents and there is a restraining order on the father. And the good news is, the father is in a rehab center, being helped with his addictions. We pushed and pushed until that critical next step was taken. Then, we found Harold a mentor here at school, one of our retired teachers who has been involved in the local writer's society for years. While she was working with him in Mrs. Cantrell's English class, she discovered that he has a real knack for storytelling."

"What happened next?"

"Well, we've been turning the students at all three sites loose to explore their creative passions, and we're seeing all kinds of outflow from this shift of focus. We've had kids of all ages reveal hidden gifts and interests most of our staff didn't know they had. So, each afternoon, we're setting aside time in each room for students to share their creativity. Then, on Fridays, we have a showcase for the whole school to enjoy. At one of these gatherings, Harold told a funny story about his granddaddy that had us all rolling in the floor with laughter."

"How did he get from that point to winning a regional writing award?"

"His mentor and Mrs. Cantrell were helping him one day with a writing assignment, and it's like he just took off. Apparently, he had been preoccupied for so long with just surviving the dysfunctional culture at home that he had suppressed this innate ability he has to tell stories. Oh, for sure, we're going to have to go slow in helping him to learn to write grammatically, but I'm telling you, John, his stories jump off the page—just as gripping as they are when he's telling them."

"Wonder where he gets it?"

"Well, we have found out that the grandfather I mentioned is known down at the old town square for his gift of weaving a story while loafing with his friends, and his other papaw was a country preacher. So, it does run in his genes, apparently."

"And you found it all because of a schoolwide focus on your students sharing their creative juices? So you set aside time every afternoon for this exploring of art, music, storytelling, creative writing? I love it, Brad."

"Drama, crafts, sewing, crocheting, scrapbooking, woodworking—it keeps growing every week, John. And the volunteers are so excited about it! Honestly, they're the ones who made it happen."

"I bet your student attendance has shot through the roof!"

"Yes, indeed. And we've got students from neighboring districts on a waiting list to enroll in our school. I can't help but believe that it's largely due to this focus on daily creativity. The word on kids enjoying school travels fast in parent circles."

"You left one area out, Brad. Why isn't physical education included in this exploration of creativity?"

"Oh, it is. We start each morning with warm-up exercises in every room or walking outside, if the weather permits. Then, the last thirty minutes of the day, knowing the kids are tired and their brains are tired too, we wrap up with free play. If it's warm, we're outside playing kickball, wiffleball, soccer, volleyball, or camp games, throwing Frisbees, jumping rope, walking the perimeter of the property, whatever. The teachers take turns planning the activities and supervising, and our volunteers love to help, too."

"And the high schoolers have bought into this?"

"Oh, John, yes! I'm seeing the 'little boy and little girl' come out again in some who had become so withdrawn and stressed with the thought of having to be adults all of a sudden."

"What if it's too cold or rainy to go outside?"

"We do some more stretches and calisthenics, and then we pull out the learning games."

"Learning games?"

"You know, chess, checkers, Scrabble, dominoes, Monopoly, Uno, things like that. You should see this place, John. The whole building is filled with students in every little cubbyhole and hallway, playing, but also learning and sharpening their thinking skills."

"And your teachers don't mind?"

"Mind? Quite the opposite. They say they can tell a difference in how the kids perform in the traditional disciplines since we implemented the creativity and exercise focus in the afternoons."

John shook his head as he looked at the floor and laughed as if he'd just found a gold mine. "Creativity, working with the hands, music, storytelling, exercise, group fun outside, learning games inside—sounds like what you'd guess children of all ages would need developmentally and would absolutely love. Yet, you won't find this on a daily basis in almost any school in our modern culture, Brad. And I can't tell you why. It's as if we lost our way and haven't been able to get back home. But Smith School is an exception. You have definitely found home."

In *Best Practice: New Standards for Teaching and Learning in America's Schools*, Steven Zemelman, Harvey Daniels, and Arthur Hyde (1998) explore in detail how the classroom can make each discipline come alive, including the arts. The authors recommend creative arts experiences be integrated into the curriculum as a major emphasis and supported by all teachers, not just arts specialists.

Summary

Smith School comes alive when the faculty commits daily time to student exercise and the exploration of individual creativity. Attendance shoots up, teachers appreciate how engaged the students are all day long, and parents from surrounding school districts increasingly inquire about enrolling their children in Smith School.

Reflection:

1. What is your school's philosophy on the creative arts?
2. What is your school's philosophy on student exercise and fitness?
3. What is your school's philosophy on students and staff sharing their creativity in an integrated classroom setting? (For example, would a student who plays the banjo have the opportunity to perform in class at times other than the end-of-year talent show?)

CHAPTER SEVENTEEN

~

Learning at Home

The scholars looked and looked outward for the answer, in far away places and with huge fiscal investments. One day, a peasant from the town joined their conversation. "You're looking for something that cannot be found 'out there'. The answer you treasure is right here at home, and the townspeople who have found it will not need your permission anymore."

The end of February brought with it a flu that swept through Smithtown, and when John came by for his regular visit, he was surprised that Brad was not distressed. "I figured you'd be all gloom and doom, Brad. I heard on the radio that all three of your centers are out for the rest of the week."

"Yes, back in the old days, John, we'd have been scrambling trying to figure out how to make these days up, what it was costing the district, and so on. But with this new four-day week, and how much we've learned to tap into the resources at home, the days the kids spend actually here in our buildings are so much less significant."

"How do you mean?"

"Well, from the start, we made sure that the Mondays we were off were used for carefully planned homework, field trips, clubs, and for other projects. So, our students are already conditioned to use their time wisely regarding school responsibilities. And with the capabilities of the Internet, the home is now becoming the 'school away from school' in many ways."

"So you're actually giving students homework to do online?"

"Oh mercy, yes, John. And Dr. Cobb has been so impressed with the whole Smith School model, he's asked me to survey our parents to find out who doesn't have Internet access at home, and he and the board are helping to purchase laptops for those families. This changes everything for us in terms of the flexibility we have to extend our school beyond these walls."

"Do you actually have teachers working online with students?"

"Yes, we're doing that, and I'm even teaching my life skills class online some. It's amazing what research the students have access to on the Internet."

"Do they send you assignments online?"

"Sure, and I have them doing some small-group work as well. They absolutely love the interaction with each other."

"But how do you regulate the quality of their work, Brad? Isn't there a great temptation to take shortcuts?"

"Well, that was one of my main concerns when we started exploring this route earlier this year. But John, I have found that if I am willing to put some time into it, assuring the quality of work is no different than it would be at school. In fact, we're seeing evidence that the kids spend much more time doing their assignments online at home than they had been at school. They've been raised on technology, unlike our generation. So, what might seem like drudgery in our traditional modes of classroom instruction becomes very interesting for the kids when we empower them to do it with the Internet."

"Isn't it a barrier not having the students actually physically in the classroom with you?"

"I thought it would be, but really, once I get to know the kids here at school in our regular classroom format, it doesn't slow us down at all if part of the work is being done online. And with the requirement to share what they've been reading and studying through reflections, I actually get far more total participation in our online work than I would ever get in face-to-face sessions."

"This is amazing, Brad. So right now, you have teachers and students from all three of your centers working at home as if they were on computers here at school, and both the teachers and the students enjoy it?"

"Yes. And the parents love it, too. For the first time, they actually get to see firsthand just what is being covered in class, and they can assist as needed. I have one dad who's a Civil War enthusiast who has collaborated with his son all winter on a history project that began as an assignment here at school. I have a mom who's helping with a classroom project online that includes helping a group of students with scrapbooking."

"But how is she pulling that off, since there's so much 'hands on' involved in scrapbooking?"

"Well, she has that particular group set up so they can participate in live chats, and she's doing some video for them that they can view online."

"Wouldn't it be neat, Brad, if you could make a video here at school that all of your staff and students could watch online?"

"We've done that a few times this year already."

"Can students do this, too?"

"Oh yes, John. You should see some of the productions they're posting on their blogs, things that were generated by class work or assignments here at school. And the PowerPoint presentations—wow! You should see some of the creations the students in my life skills class have developed this year. Some great, great stuff."

"Brad, I had just never taken the time to think through this whole concept of students using technology to learn at home. When I have read about instructional technology, I've thought of two conduits—students working on computers at school, and online classes offered by the state department and other agencies that allow students to pursue independent learning that might not be offered in their regular school curriculum."

"And we do have students taking those types of courses, too, John. We have students who were ready for more advanced work learning with tutors online in courses in math and science, for example. But we also have students who need extra remedial help seeing success with this same mode of delivery."

"Brad, this gives your four-day week even more merit, if you have this entire school community so engaged in independent learning at home."

"Yes, it totally redefines the traditional school week, John. Actually, it redefines the entire school year. We're already looking into a summer school model that will be almost completely online, except for a few sessions here at school and some nice field trips for the students."

"Makes sense. Solves a dilemma we've struggled with for the last thirty years, Brad—how to provide effective instruction over the summer months. Do you envision some of your other students taking advantage of this option as well?"

"Yes, we do. Why would we close down shop all summer if we have kids who would like to take a course or two online? We already have several high school students who are asking if they can help develop more courses. And some of them are already spending part of their school day with the elementary and middle school levels, tutoring and helping with classroom technology."

"Brad, this conversation makes me think of when the automobile came along, and the television. No matter how scared some people were of these wild new technologies, after a while, their advantages just made too much sense. And they transformed the culture of those eras."

"Good analogies, John. And with school, I see these new tools as resources that we have barely tapped. So many of the problems we have faced over the years in how to prepare every child for a productive, fulfilling life could be addressed more effectively if we will keep exploring beyond our past paradigms. Yes, it's stepping into deep, uncharted waters. But it seems to me the potential is worth the risk. After all, our schools should be about the needs of our students—not the comfort zones of adults."

"Brad, I couldn't have said it better myself. Now, you've piqued my interest. Show me what your online life skills course looks like. Better yet, may I jump into one of the discussions with your students? You know how I love to philosophize!"

"You bet! They'd love it!"

In *Future Perfect*, Stanley M. Davis (1987) provides a glimpse into the future of organizations that illustrates the absolute necessity of tearing down old walls of tradition and habit and replacing them with new paradigms that reshape how we use the essential raw materials of time, space, and matter.

Summary

Smithtown is hit with the winter flu season, but John is amazed at how the school community adapts, using the Internet and distance learning technology to such a degree that the home becomes an extension of the classroom. Brad explains that with the new four-day week, teachers and students have been tapping into this flexibility to do some school projects and assignments online from home, even before the flu closed the school.

Reflection:

1. How well is your school integrating the Internet and distance learning into daily and weekly instruction?
2. What structure, space, and time barriers stand in the way of your school's master schedule being reinvented to better meet the needs of your students?
3. What "paradigm locks" in your community present obstacles to needed changes to the traditional brick-and-mortar and six-hour-day system of schooling?

CHAPTER EIGHTEEN

~

Advisor-Advisee

Mentoring is more than giving directions. Mentoring is shepherding, and teaching the student about the all of life, and what it means to be prepared to live it well.

John had been pleasantly surprised when Linda called and volunteered her school, Heritage Elementary, for his next principals cohort meeting. She said her principal had said it was fine, and that she wanted to sit in if that was okay. Linda was John's first assignment as a principal mentor, and she had had an amazing first year in leading a school. But after that initial year, she had decided to go back to the classroom, at least for a while, since her children were still small. She met John at the door of the school with a smile and a hug.

"John, I hear so many great things about your program. And now it's spreading across the state. I'm so proud of you!"

"Well, it's not me, Linda. It's the talented school leaders like you that I am privileged to work with who are making the difference. I'm glad you're going to sit in today, I've mentioned you to this group. They will be glad to finally get to meet you."

After introductions, John asked for a sharing of 'what's working, what's not.' When the last principal was to speak, she simply said, "They're not robots. They're people—just like you and me. And many are still children in adult bodies."

"Hi, Stephanie," John said. "Glad you could make it today. I agree completely with your statement, and we'd like to hear more of your perspectives.

Go on." John was gentle with this group. He worked to help them to be transparent and vulnerable, so they could give and receive support. He loved it when the conversation shifted from exterior to the heart.

Stephanie stood up, wiped her eyes with shaking hands, and continued, "We lost a girl a couple of weeks ago. I don't mean she ran away for a day or two. She took her own life, whether on purpose or accidentally we'll never know. And as I listened these last few days to the grief all around me from her family, her friends, and her teachers, I just wanted to disappear."

Stephanie sobbed as she looked around the table, needing desperately to warn her colleagues to take the necessary steps to avoid what she was going through. "You see, this girl, Katie, had been hanging by a thread for the longest time, and I just kept putting off and putting off what I knew we needed at our high school. She used to be a straight-A student, but her parents got divorced a couple of years ago, and the next thing we knew, she did a complete one-eighty. She started running with a different crowd, her grades dropped, she started skipping classes, and she became a heavy drinker. They found her car in the river, her body in it."

John gently prodded her for more information. "Help me to understand better, Stephanie. *What* had you realized you needed at your school?" John knew how hard this was for Stephanie, but he also knew it was so important for her to get this out and to come to better closure.

"A support system for our kids."

"Did your counselors not know that Katie was in trouble?"

"Sure they did, and they tried to help. But it was too little, too late. I attended a session at a school leadership conference last summer that explained step-by-step how to start an effective advisor-advisee program, and I had this model on my list of important things to do this school year. But, as is so often the case, I didn't follow up with it because it wasn't another urgent fire to put out."

"Tell us more about this advisor-advisee concept, Stephanie." John realized that Stephanie was not the only one in the room who had been too busy to implement needed change in their school. This was a great opportunity to dig deeper in a way that would help all of them.

Stephanie took a deep breath. "It's a powerful avenue for extending the total menu of services far past the core courses. And it only takes an hour or less a week. But if you train your staff and then develop the curriculum you know the students are not getting enough of, pretty soon, the kids are being given some important coaching from their assigned advisors about all kinds of real-life issues. They can meet with their advisors in homeroom, after lunch, the last thirty minutes of the day, or on club day—there are different ways to make it work."

Someone yelled, "There's just not enough time!" Several heads nodded in agreement.

Stephanie did not waver. "But so much of what we are pushing to the fringe—everything from nutrition and health issues, to time management, to filling out applications for college—can be covered in advisor-advisee. The topics are limitless. And guest speakers and volunteers from the local community can help, too."

"Sounds a lot like my life skills class," Brad said. He explained more about the course he was facilitating for his juniors and seniors, and how Millie had been developing an advisor-advisee model for both high school and middle school students at Smith School.

"That's wonderful, Brad," said Stephanie. "And in Katie's situation, just maybe some focused teaching early on about the realities of alcohol would have made a difference. Her advisor could have provided some one-to-one coaching, too, when she first noticed Katie starting to slide. The key is being proactive, not reactive. Why do we assume our teenagers aren't struggling with complicated issues? Or maybe it's just that we don't know how to provide a safety net for them, so we bury our heads in the sand."

As Stephanie sat down, her hands were still trembling. She continued, "Doesn't a program like this make so much more sense than expecting our counselors to somehow be able to handle their workloads and delicate student personal issues, too? We only have two or three counselors in a high school of a few hundred kids. It's ridiculous that we expect them to have the time to meet all of the emotional and other needs our students have at this age."

John nodded. "I agree, Stephanie. You've identified another part of the system that's been broken for a long, long time." John could tell the whole group had much to say and personal experiences to share about the lack of resources to help students with the 'basics of life,' as one in the group later put it.

Before the session was over, every participant had jotted down the e-mail address Stephanie had brought with her for learning more about how to create an effective advisor-advisee program. A couple of principals whose schools had already implemented advisor-advisee admitted that they needed to develop their models further.

John closed by adding, "Today, perhaps you folks took the first step in saving many more Katies that are right now walking the halls of your schools. Let's discuss your progress on advisor-advisee next month, too. Let's make sure we don't let Stephanie's plea get put on the shelf. Now's the time to put the item on your agenda for the rest of the spring."

As the group dispersed and headed back to their schools, Linda stayed behind and asked John if she could talk to him for a minute. "John, I've had a lot of time to think these last two years. It's been wonderful to be back in the classroom, and oh mercy me, I've used the leadership and relationship principles you and I used to talk about in our mentoring chats so, so much with my students. But my own kids are a little older now, and my husband's work allows him to have a lot of flexibility with his hours each week. So, after a lot of praying, I've decided to go back into the principalship."

"Linda, that's wonderful! I knew you'd go back to the hot seat someday." Both laughed, and John shook Linda's hand firmly.

"Well, it won't be easy, John. I remember my first year. But I also realize that what these schools need most is principled shepherds who care deeply about the kids, the staff, and the entire school community. I know I can make a difference, and while I am still young and willing, it's time to do it. Maybe just for four or five years. We'll see."

John nodded and asked, "The next question is, where do you think there might be an opening that you'd be suited for?"

Linda just smiled, and her eyes welled up with tears. "The principal who replaced me here has done such a fantastic job. He built on the programs we had put in place, John, and the strong culture. And the students and staff have such great respect for him too. But he called me into his office last week and told me he'd been offered a school closer to his hometown, and he was going to take it. He'll be leaving at the end of June. He also told me that he'd be honored if I'd consider taking the vacancy. And he said he'd gotten hints from the faculty this week that they hoped I would be given the opportunity."

"Linda, I am absolutely thrilled for you, and for this school."

"And John, like you always say, first things first. So when school's out, my husband and I are taking the kids on a long vacation, and then I'm going to do what Brad told me you taught him to do last fall. I'm getting away from my school work for a few days with my family every quarter. And I'm going to be so on top of my management of priorities and resources that there will be no more of those twelve- and fourteen-hour days that wore me out the first time. On weekends, I'm going to really be home—not mentally and emotionally back at school. I've made that promise to myself and to my family. This school's going to be about quality, but also balance. And not just for me—I'm going to help my staff to learn this core value, too."

"Will you do me a favor, Linda, sometime later this spring?"

"Sure."

"Come over to Smith School, and spend a day with Brad. I think he's got a model that's just what the doctor ordered."

In *Heart to Heart: Awakenings*, Carol Christian and Rocky Wallace (2009) share scenarios from the classroom that point to the critical need for teachers and schools to be focused on student needs that go beyond classroom performance.

Summary

During a cohort session, a principal shares how much she regrets not being proactive in implementing an advisor-advisee program for her high school students. A girl from her school has died due to alcohol abuse, and the danger signs had been evident for several weeks.

Reflection:

1. What student support systems do you have in your school?
2. How does your school take a proactive stance in helping students to make smarter choices and avoid poor ones?
3. What training has your school staff had in creating a comprehensive and effective menu of services that goes beyond academics? Are volunteers and partners from the community engaged in this effort?

CHAPTER NINETEEN

~

A Child's Goodbye

This journey down here is but a vapor, as we make our way back home. It's not how long we stay, but how we treat those traveling with us along the way.

As March ushered in the final weeks of the school year, John dropped in to chat with Brad one more time before spring break. Millie was sitting in Brad's office with her head in her hands, and John could tell she was upset.

"It's one of our middle school students, John," Brad explained. "She's dying of cancer."

"When did you find out?"

"Well, her parents told us several months ago that something was wrong, but the doctors thought they had it under control. But this morning, her mother called. It looks like this will be her last spring with us. Her mom wants her to finish out the school year with her classmates, and we're just trying to decide how to approach this."

Millie's hands trembled as she wept. "How did you handle a dying child, John, when you were a principal?"

"To be honest, Millie, I've never experienced something like this before. We did have a maintenance man who died in a farming accident while still on staff in our district, and we lost a set of parents one time in a house fire. Those were very hard situations for the school and the community. Both times, the love and support that poured out to the families of the victims was tremendous. With a child, though, it will be different. I think the main thing is to celebrate with her these very special days ahead. By the way, what is her name?"

"Shannon," Millie said. "Shannon Watson. She's a seventh grader, and just as sweet as sweet can be. I want you to meet her, John. She knows what's going on. May I go get her?" Millie looked at John with pleading, swollen eyes, and he nodded.

A couple of minutes later, Millie brought Shannon into Brad's office. Brad stood up and walked over to shake the girl's hand. "Shannon, this is my coach, much like your teachers mentor and coach you in your classes. John, this is Shannon, one of the best kids I have ever worked with in my life." Brad's voice broke and he cleared his throat to disguise his struggle to remain composed.

"Hello, sir. It's a privilege to meet you. I guess you've heard I'm pretty sick."

"Yes, ma'am, I have. Brad and Millie, I mean Mr. Williamson and Mrs. Thompson, have shared with me that you have something pretty complicated. I think it's absolutely wonderful that you're able to come to school every day and be here with your friends and your teachers."

"Oh, I wouldn't have it any other way, sir. My parents have been so, so sweet during all of this, and they asked me what I wanted to do. I want to live each day just like I always have. Why would I want to stay home watching TV or staying in bed all day? Besides, I believe in miracles, and I have faith that I just may turn the corner. If that would happen, think how far behind I'd be next year!"

John swallowed hard and pinched his leg for several seconds so he could remain calm and composed. He didn't want Shannon to see him cry in the middle of a conversation with her.

"I think you're exactly right, Shannon. Let me ask you something: what would you want to happen here at school these last few weeks of the school year? I agree with you, you might indeed get better. I have faith that all things are possible, and that prayers are answered every day that cannot be explained by anything but a miracle. I have heard doctors acknowledge this, too. But, in the meantime, you will never have a better opportunity to have Mr. Williamson and Mrs. Thompson's attention. What would you tell them they should think about doing for the remainder of the school year?"

Shannon thought for a moment, with her finger on her chin. "Hmm, let's see. Well, I'd love for an orchestra from a big town to come here to school to play. I think that would be the coolest thing for little Smithtown!" Shannon laughed as she thought of the possibility, and Millie scrambled to find a pen to start taking notes.

"Great idea! What else?" John saw Brad smile, and he knew he and Millie were on the same page with him all the way.

"Gee, this is fun! Well, I'd love for us to have a day this spring when the whole school went out into the community and did good deeds for people, especially the older folks who might need chores taken care of or groceries brought home. Wouldn't that be a wonderful way for us to give back to the community after the wonderful year they've given us?"

"I think that's a wonderful idea, too, Shannon. And I wonder why I didn't think of that way back when I was a principal. Keep going."

Shannon grinned. "This is awesome. Okay, let's see . . . what about a day set aside for honoring our custodians? They keep the school so clean, but I bet they hardly ever get told so. And what about a day like this for our cooks, too, with the food catered in? They could just enjoy all of us on that day. You know, visit classrooms, walk around the school and see what's going on. I bet not one time have they ever done that, since they're always cooking and waiting on us, from before daylight until afternoon when they clean up."

"Shannon, I needed you as my assistant when I was a principal!" John exclaimed. "I never thought of those ideas either, and they're marvelous gestures of kindness. What about your classes? Anything new to make them more special as the spring unfolds?"

"Just let me write, and be creative in art class, and sing without worrying about the notes so much in chorus. And let me play my flute in band without correcting me as often. I love my teachers, but I think some times they worry so much about our state tests, they seem to be on pins and needles. I wonder what it would be like if we explored more in all our classes? Don't get me wrong, we have been doing more this year than ever before. And to be honest, those are the times the kids love school the most."

"When you're exploring?"

"When we're learning for the joy of learning, without pressure all the time."

"Any special field trips?"

"Yes. I'd love to take a long, half-day hike down a beautiful trail. Maybe my PE or science class could do that this year. I've been to the mall all my life, and I can rent videos every weekend. But for me, when I'm out in nature, something moves inside that I can't explain."

"Shannon, these are all such excellent suggestions. Have we left anything out?"

"One more thing. On our last day this year, could we honor our parents? Instead of me being brought up front for an award, I'd like to surprise Mom and Dad and have them brought up to receive the recognition. After all, they're the support behind the scenes that has made all the difference."

Millie turned away, unable to hold back the tears any longer. Brad thanked Shannon for coming down to meet John and for giving him an amazing list of things that would make the spring the best end of year ever for Smith School.

Shannon headed out the door of Brad's office, then she stopped and turned back. "Just one more request, Mr. Williamson."

Brad's voice cracked—he couldn't hide his emotion anymore, either. "Yes, Shannon. What is it?"

"I've been working on something special that I would like you to read to my friends and family if I'm too sick to come back to school. I'll bring it by next week, and I'd like you to not let anyone see it until I'm gone, you know, if I don't get better after all. Would you do that for me?"

Brad rushed to the door and gave Shannon the longest hug. "I sure will, little girl. It would be an honor."

In *The Shaping School Culture Fieldbook*, Kent D. Peterson and Terrence E. Deal (2002) provide insight into the all-important domain of school culture. The culture of any school is layered with values, history, and rituals, and creating a culture that is positive and healthy for all stakeholders is critical to the school's effectiveness.

Summary

When a middle school student is stricken with a terminal illness, John, Brad, and Millie are moved as the girl shares how she would love to see her last semester play out. Her creative ideas point to a culture more focused on the celebration of learning, not the endless assessment of learning, and give Brad several clues on relationship-driven school improvement from a student's perspective.

Reflection:

1. What would you do for students at your school if you could go "outside the lines" and plan a variety of engaging, enjoyable activities?
2. How would you describe your school's work culture? For students? For staff?
3. How would your students rate the relationship IQ of your school?

CHAPTER TWENTY

~

Kids Know—But Do We Listen?

The most honest people in our lives are children. If we will but slow down long enough, they will share with us simple words of wisdom that can help us in our yearning to make the world a better place.

Brad cried all the way home that evening, and the first thing he did when he got to his front door was run upstairs to his kids' bedrooms.

"Paige? Barry? Where are Daddy's Little Princess and Little Man?"

Brad's kids both came running down the hall as he reached the top of the stairs, and he hugged them tightly as they jumped up into his arms. "Oh, how I love these two jewels that are such a blessing to Mommy and Daddy's lives! Here, sit on the stairs and talk to me for a minute. Tell me what you like most about school."

Paige, who was seven, squinted her eyes and thought hard. "Mainly, Daddy, I like school the best when we make things and work with our hands. And I love it when my teacher reads us stories. She gathers us around her at our reading center, sits in her rocking chair, and everything just feels so cozy and safe. And I like it when she has us work in the other centers, too. It seems a lot like home, and how you and Mommy always have creative things for us to do. And Daddy, I like it a lot when my teachers know my name and talk to me about stuff. When they're friendly, I relax and don't feel homesick. But when someone's grumpy, it makes the whole class feel sad."

Brad smiled. "What about you, Barry? What are your favorite times at school?"

The five-year-old smiled sheepishly, fiddled with his hands, and simply said, "Play. When we play, Daddy, school is fun, and I don't want to miss."

"Tell me, little guy, how do you play?"

"With blocks . . . in the sandbox . . . with clay . . . with games . . . outside at recess . . . and in PE class."

"Are you learning to read, Barry?"

"Oh yeah, that too. I almost forgot. Yes, Daddy, I am so glad I'm learning to read. I want to read for you again tonight after supper, okay?"

"Yes, sir! You've got a deal! Anything you don't like about school, Barry?"

"Nope! I love all of it! . . . Well, there is one thing, Daddy. I don't like getting up in the dark in the winter. It's too early, and I think schools should remember we little people need our rest and need to be home with Mommy when it's still nighttime."

Brad laughed as he reached over and tickled Barry's knee. "I agree, Bear. Whoever thought up the notion of little kids getting up and catching the bus before daylight anyway?"

"I thought you did, Daddy!" Barry reached over and tickled Brad back, and the two rolled on the floor, laughing.

"What about you, Sis? Is there anything that my little Paige would change at school if you could?"

"Just one thing, Daddy."

"Now what would that one thing be?"

"I wish the computer man wasn't so mean."

"What do you mean?"

"When we go to the computer lab on Tuesday mornings, none of us really want to go because Mr. Wickers is so grumpy all the time."

"You mean Mr. Vickers. What do you mean he's grumpy? Mr. Vickers is the best technology teacher we've had around here in a long time."

"But Daddy, he yells at kids when they mess up. And he makes class so stressful, none of us like it."

"Tell you what I'll do. I'll look into it. Maybe Mr. Vickers has a lot going on, and the morning you're in his class, he's distracted with other work he'll need to complete that day. Is there anything else that you don't like about school?"

"Just when we get interrupted or a class gets cancelled. One time this year, Daddy, we missed art class for three straight weeks! And sometimes, when we go to music, we get there late or something has been scheduled so we have to leave early. I don't like it when school gets so busy and hectic. I can tell it makes the teachers nervous, and it makes us kids nervous, too. You and

Mommy always taught us that every day is a gift, so we shouldn't rush it away. But sometimes, at school it's like the whole point is to rush the day away."

Brad blushed as he wondered about his own frantic work habits at school. "And, Daddy, one day last week, one of our volunteer grandparents came in to do math with us, and there was so little time, we just skipped it. I felt sorry for him. He's so good and sweet, and he helps us understand math better, too."

Brad looked at the wall, frustrated with the realization that even a seven-year-old can pick up on the fact that the flow of the school day is critical. "Tell you what guys, let's go get Mommy and run out for some ice cream, then a walk in the park. I think it's time for one of our evenings when it's just family and nothing else."

"Yeah!!!" Barry and Paige squealed, jumping on Brad and knocking him over. And he realized that this was his first responsibility—right here at home, in the loving arms of his family.

> In *The Art of the Long View*, Peter Schwartz (1996) explains why scenario building is such an important piece of organizational improvement. As we plan strategically for an innovative future, what fresh perspectives provide clues to what that future could look like?

Summary

Brad comes home one evening and chats with his two kids, a five-year-old boy and a seven-year-old girl. As he asks simple questions about what they like about school, they give him invaluable clues to what is connecting and what is missing in the school's life from a child's perspective.

Reflection:

1. How does your school's daily routine flow?
2. Would a student describe your school's culture as pleasant and enjoyable, similar to summer camp or the YMCA?
3. If not, how would a student describe your school's culture?

CHAPTER TWENTY-ONE

~

Addressing the Unfriendly Spirit

"My teacher sure is smart, Mommy, but she's also awfully sad, and sometimes mean. Wonder why she decided to become a teacher? She seems to hate it so."

April and the beginning of spring brought with it the urge to spend an evening at a farm pond, and John invited Brad to go with him. As they stood on the bank, casting rubber salamander lures beneath trees dripping softly from a gentle rain, Brad decided to ask John how he would handle the situation of the grumpy teacher.

"John, after one of my own kids innocently brought it to my attention, I have been doing some discreet checking at school, and it seems very clear that I have a teacher who is out of control sometimes with his tone of voice and how he treats our kids."

John was surprised. "That doesn't sound like your school. Is he a sub or new this semester?"

"No, and I'm frustrated that I didn't know about this sooner. We hired Jeff last summer, and everyone sang his praises all year, telling me all about how much he can do with technology. But now I'm finding out that while he is great at teaching the staff new technology skills, he is much too abrasive, even rude at times, with students."

"What level does he teach?"

"We have him spending chunks of time at all three centers. And even our high schoolers say that he's too rough and not easy to get to know."

"What do you have to show him from your classroom walkthroughs?"

"Well, that's just it. I've been so busy with the core content teachers, I haven't spent much time at all with our special area folks."

"Well, here's your opportunity. If I were you, I'd do a lot of walkthroughs for the remainder of this year, so the staff will realize that these are going to be routine next year. Use a one-page observation chart to record what you see. Then, from these observations and other types of documentation, I'd begin having one-to-one conversations with every teacher on staff each quarter. These don't have to be long sessions, but they do need to include dialogue about what's going well and what needs more attention."

"Four times a year?"

"Yep. And the staff should be helping develop their personal growth plans with you directly from these charts. Don't just zero in on weaknesses, include genuine praise with specific examples. You'll be amazed, Brad, how much this one coaching strategy will improve the quality of teaching in your school. The staff will get used to this ongoing feedback and they'll embrace it."

"If you'll help me get comfortable with this, I'll start doing it, John. Sounds like a 'win, win' for all of us in moving toward a customized staff development model."

"You'll see a positive difference, Brad. Don't just limit it to your certified staff, either. Use it as an improvement tool with your classified staff as well. And, to be honest, you need to be working with your supervisor, the super-intendent, on a personal growth plan for yourself."

"Yes, I realize that. If I want my team at school to buy in to this, they'll need to know that I am being held accountable by the very same process."

"Have you talked with your teacher Jeff yet about his tone of voice with his students?"

"Actually, John, I brought it up very gingerly yesterday. I had the op-portunity to sit down with him for lunch at school, and I worked student relationships into the conversation. Honestly, it went right over his head. He kept going on and on about how immature kids are, and how if they would just listen, he could teach them twice as fast as he has been going. I finally dropped it, and that's why I thought you might have an idea or two."

"Well, you're wise not to ignore it. Way too many kids will share later that a teacher or two was too much subject-driven and too little relationship-driven. And sometimes, a teacher will not be strong in either area. It's the principal's job to help the teacher address these and any other such gaps. If not, the students are the victims—perhaps for years and years, if the teacher decides to stay in the profession."

"Oh, I think Jeff is strong in his knowledge of content. But I don't think he understands the relationship factor that you speak of. How do I even begin to help him learn to be nice to his students, John? Aren't we sort of permanently wired to get along well with people and treat them right or are we not wired that way?

"No, actually, we're not permanently wired that way, Brad. Remember the EI skills I've worked on with your staff? All of us can develop stronger emotional intelligence. How we interact, inspire, communicate, listen, even how we read the other person's mood and respond can be taken to a more effective level. EI is not simply people skills, although that's a big part of it."

"So, my dad, who's always had an amazing humility about him that makes others feel at ease, even though he has mastered everything he ever tried, is strong in EI."

"Most likely."

"And my mom, who never met a stranger and who makes the room light up whenever she walks in, is also strong in EI."

"Most likely."

"And I seem to be almost able to read the minds of my staff and students when they come to me with issues—I probably inherited strong EI as well."

"Perhaps. But remember, it can be learned and improved upon. And oh my, it makes life so much simpler, because we are in tune with the feelings and emotions of those all around us, and are able to connect, whether as their spouse, parent, friend, supervisor, colleague, in whatever capacity. So someone like Jeff, who has the technical skills,but struggles with how he communicates empathy and respect for his students, may or may not be suited for the teaching profession. It will depend on how serious he is about improving his EI. And that's where you come in."

"What should I do first?"

"I'd start the walkthroughs we've discussed immediately, then begin the one-to-one coaching sessions. As soon as you can, it would be helpful to you and your staff for you to find a conference on EI, and take Jeff and some others with you. Then, as follow-up to my training earlier this year, to hold you all accountable on this in the long term, build in EI discussions and further training for every team in your school for this summer and fall."

"Will this plan help Jeff to be more gentle with kids?"

"We sure hope so. By next year this time, you'll know whether Jeff is getting it or not. If he shows improvement in his EI, you've perhaps salvaged a career. If he doesn't, you and Dr. Cobb will need to help him move on to another career where he doesn't work with children and youth. It's really pretty simple when you break it down to what's best for the students who are entrusted to your care."

"Thanks, John. Sounds like a plan that will benefit every staffer at Smith School and, ultimately, our students." Just then, Brad hooked into a lunker bass that fought him for a good three minutes. When he finally dragged the fish up on the bank, he had landed a six-pound largemouth! John took pictures, Brad released the big granddaddy, and they both stopped talking school and got down to business—fishing a farm pond during a gentle spring rain.

In *Coaching People*, Harvard Business School Press (2006) details doable strategies for one-to-one coaching conversations that can lead to individual and organizational improvement.

Summary

Brad investigates Paige's complaint further and discovers that his technology teacher is not connecting with his students, but instead is harsh and abrasive. John suggests that Brad implement a system of ongoing classroom walkthroughs and an individual growth plan process for all staff at Smith School that includes regular one-to-one conversations with Brad. John also recommends following up on the emotional intelligence training he had provided the Smith School staff earlier in the year.

Reflection:

1. Do you have any staff who are abrasive or insensitive to students?
2. Are all staff on an ongoing individual growth plan with regular performance conversations with their supervisor, and customized training provided as needed?
3. Do you have any staff who are misplaced—skilled in one or more areas, but not currently working in those areas of expertise?

CHAPTER TWENTY-TWO

~

Talent and Potential versus Flaws and Failure

Tell me I'm doing well when I am doing well. Please notice. I'm human, and I need to hear that you have realized my unique gifts. Then, I am coachable, because you have offered me kindness instead of scorn, authentic relationship instead of control.

Brad was busy helping Millie make last-minute preparations for talent week, a showcase that had evolved out of the increased emphasis on integrating students' creative interests into their daily studies.

"Wow, Brad," John exclaimed when he stopped in, "this place is alive with excitement! I saw your sign out front. Are all three schools involved in a talent week focus?"

"Yes," Brad replied. "And we've got lots of folks from the community coming in to share their unique gifts as well, John. This is kind of a capstone project, an extension of our daily focus on individual strengths and creative interests; the momentum for it has been growing all year. You can walk into any of our centers on any given day at any given time and you'll find someone playing a guitar, or reading a creative composition, or illustrating how to take care of a horse farm or make a quilt. The kids love it, the parents love it, the teachers love it, and the community's more engaged in Smith School than ever before."

"Brad, I am increasingly impressed with the transformational culture of this school. The creative climate, the celebration of individual uniqueness, and the focus on active learning is definitely a model for the future. Your students must just shine in this environment. It makes me think of when my kids were little, and they would go to summer camp or to special classes at the YMCA, or to their granddaddy's farm. They would come back from those experiences so renewed, and so happy and self-confident because they had learned by doing."

"You've explained it well, John. Yes, our kids do love it. Our average daily attendance keeps climbing higher than it's ever been, and we have practically no discipline issues. Students make it a point to come and tell me that school has never been this fun. The teachers are telling me that teaching has never been so fulfilling. They, too, are absent less than ever in the past, and they are embracing this model of learning. And I am seeing more technology used in the classroom this year, by far, than I used to see."

"And the teachers are sharing their hobbies and other talents just like the kids are doing?"

"Sure are. In reality, it's very similar to how you explain your children's happiest learning experiences. Smith School is more like summer camp or the YMCA. And John, it makes so much sense, and we're seeing such fantastic results, I would never go back to the conventional way of doing school. No wonder the staff were burned out, the kids were tired of school by the time they reached third grade, and the community tried to avoid us. The traditional 'sit and get' model of learning that we all bought into for so long was a very sterile, factory-like place to be.

"Would any adult enjoy such an environment day after day at work? Of course not!" Brad drew closer, lowering his voice to a whisper. "I see now why some students used to refer to school as prison. For many who didn't enjoy neat rows of chairs with the teachers doing most of the talking all day long, it was probably a daily nightmare."

John nodded. "That might explain the high dropout rates and the relatively low number of high school graduates who have gone on to complete postsecondary training, Brad. Maybe the universal system of schooling has been far more broken than we have admitted for a long, long time . . . You mentioned your teachers being renewed. How is your technology teacher doing?"

"Oh, I'm glad you asked. I wanted to update you on Jeff. I followed your suggestion, and Jeff and I have started having regular one-to-one chats about teaching and learning. It has been fascinating for me to be allowed inside the world of a technology guru. And Jeff is indeed a guru. He's bringing this school's technology IQ along, especially with our staff, in ways that I would not have thought possible last year this time."

"How did he respond to your concerns about his lack of emotional intelligence in teacher-student communication and building healthy relationships?"

"He was very quiet at first, almost as if he was embarrassed to talk about it. But gradually, he's opened up, and we've had some wonderful talks about his strengths and areas that need more attention. The bottom line, John, is that Jeff needs to be working primarily with the adults at all three of our Smith School centers, and also used in other ways to develop state-of-the-art instructional technology. We have him spread too thin, going to all three centers and working with all age groups."

"So, you don't feel that he is misplaced in the school setting?"

"No, not at all. But if we really want our technology services to grow as they need to, we do need another tech instructor who enjoys the classroom setting to team with Jeff next school year. I'm going to ask Dr. Cobb to help us make that happen. We must not neglect the potential of technology to transform the twenty-first-century classroom. And we can't overload Jeff and then blame him because he is not capable of doing everything Smith School needs all by himself."

"Sounds like those one-to-one discussions have made a huge difference."

"They have, John. I was ready to recommend that Jeff find another job this summer; I am so glad I made the time to understand him better, listen to how he feels about his work, and provide some carefully targeted coaching. And after going through this process, I'm going to line up a mentor who has a strong background in technology for Jeff this coming year. We think we know of someone in a nearby district who will lend a hand."

"Great route to take, Brad. Perhaps he and Jeff can visit each other's schools and share insights and suggestions. That way, both school districts benefit, too."

"I agree, it can be a great partnership for all of us. And I've learned from these sessions with Jeff that I need to do these chats with every person on my staff. You were right, John. So I've been doing the walkthroughs, and I've started the one-to-one coaching process. By the end of the spring semester, we'll all be used to it. It's an invaluable tool for staff development, and I don't know why I didn't think of it my first year as a principal."

"Because you were so busy putting out fires, you didn't have time to focus on the much more effective practice of preventing fires. It happens to most principals, Brad, don't beat yourself up over it."

"Well, I do know this—I have never felt better about providing the right type of support to my teachers and other staff. I now feel I am primed to empower and equip each of them. Sure feels good to know that all of us, as a team, will be focusing on our strengths and identifying areas of further growth to target, but in a positive, helpful way that promotes trust and doesn't foster the toxic habit of criticism."

"Toxic habit," said John thoughtfully. "That's a good way to put it, Brad. Isn't it so much better to build a climate that celebrates individual gifts and focuses on developing abilities than one that accepts and denies, all at the same time, that people are going to fail. Jeff is a great example. Your investing time in him and recognizing his unique contributions to the organization, instead of accepting the assumption that he might have to be replaced, not only builds trust in the relationship, it changes the rules."

"Changes the rules?" Brad asked.

"Yes. Jeff can go home in the evenings now knowing that he is valued by the organization and that you are going to provide him all the support he needs so that he can keep blooming. You see, that's so much better than some of the other routes we often take, choices that seem to foster a climate of poor performance until failure becomes a self-fulfilling prophecy. And this happens with students, too. Instead of the necessary interventions, instead of refusing to let them fail, we too often go right ahead and help them dig their graves, so to speak.

"Doesn't take long for a human being to give up on himself, if others keep pointing out his flaws but then don't provide the lifelines to correct them."

John pointed at himself. "Thinking back on my own life, my mother and father always seemed to be teaching and molding, not criticizing and scolding. What a difference that made in my self-esteem and self-confidence as a child."

"We try to do that at home with our kids too, John," said Brad. "And you're right—it makes a huge difference in how they approach life, how they embrace life. They respect it and savor it, instead of being scared of it and dreading it."

"And every classroom should have that same culture of support, discovery, and guidance, Brad. Every one."

"And I am now convinced that every teacher needs a coach, a mentor, an accountability partner of some kind, John—no matter how many years they've been in education. I cannot tell you how much I have grown as a school leader this year, and in my understanding of what an effective school should look like, just by taking the time to engage in these conversations with you. Imagine if my entire staff had such an opportunity."

"Well, your superintendent has been so impressed with the Smith School project, Brad, I'd say you have his attention if you want to bring in content area coaches for your entire staff team. Go for it."

"I will!"

In *Giving Feedback*, Harvard Business School Press (2007) suggests helpful strategies for assisting employees in overcoming obstacles and changing behavior.

Summary

John's suggestion works. Brad engages in helpful conversations with his technology teacher. As a result, the entire school benefits, as Brad is more in tune with the needs of all involved in planning professional development for the upcoming school year.

Reflection:

1. What measures have you taken to confront and assist staff who have abrasive or disconnected relationships with students, other staff, or parents?
2. Does your school have one-to-one or small-group coaching for all staff in their content areas?
3. Have you had training in coaching other personnel (other than on-the-job experience)?

CHAPTER TWENTY-THREE

~

Principles of Servant Leadership

> I watched him, the first principal I served under as a teacher, graciously and selflessly serve others day after day, year after year. He loved it. He was always good to me, always made sure the kids were made to feel special, always gently supported his staff. My first year as a principal, I found myself doing many things he had modeled for me . . . and I was proud to call him mentor. I was proud to call him friend.

As the month of May began each spring, John had always felt that he was out of time way too soon for what he still wanted to do, and this year was no exception. He almost felt guilty scheduling a final session for the principals cohort, as he knew these hardworking principals had endless tasks in these last few days of the school year. But he also knew that they would be more stressed than ever, and a couple of hours away and in the support system they had become a part of this year would be a relief they desperately needed. He had scheduled this last meeting at a steakhouse with the meal paid for.

After an hour of food and laughter, John brought the meeting to order for a time of sharing and closure. "I want to express to all of you how special this cohort has been to me. I am continually amazed at the quality of respected and gifted leaders we have serving our schools. I thought we'd go around the table and allow each of you to reflect a little on what this group has meant to you this year."

Millie held up her hand shyly, acknowledging that she would like to go first. "I cannot begin to share what being a part of this group has meant to me. Brad was nice enough to allow me to tag along. I had heard about what an effective teacher of leadership John was, and I have witnessed that first-hand this year during his work with us at Smith School.

"Just as our school year began, our former school building burned to the ground. On that Friday night, which seems like years ago now, I remember thinking that we'd fall apart and our students would scatter to the high winds." Millie's face spread into a big, wide grin. "But just the opposite has happened. We used to be a typical school, with traditions, practices, and habits that, as I look back, sometimes made so little sense. Now, we are three families of students and adults learning and growing together—a three-in-one school that is so much more than a school. We've been reborn."

Brad went next. "Before this year, I thought I had mastered what I needed to know about school leadership. After all, I had been a principal for a while, and felt like I had the whole business of schooling down pretty well. Then John was assigned to be my mentor. As we discussed the various issues, I started peeling away the layers of my assumptions about school, assumptions that don't even make sense to me now."

Brad looked down, humbled by the vulnerability and transparency John had helped him learn to embrace. "I was a good person, but I was not digging deep into my heart and servant leading as a shepherd would his flock. I was so conscious of keeping all the players happy that I was allowing a mediocre curriculum to go on, year after year, however many students it let fall through the cracks."

"I can relate, Brad, because I was a player in the big game, too." Todd scooted his chair back and stood up. "I had the good fortune to work with John as my mentor last year, and to be honest, he saved my career. People, I was drowning—burned out, washed up, praying for the day I could retire. My idea of a good school was if our ball teams won. But one day, I finally started opening my eyes and seeing all the people around me in that school who needed me to care for them. That was the main ingredient that had been missing. Once I started caring, the whole school changed."

Tears welled up in Linda's eyes, and she too stood so she could make eye contact with everyone. "I only joined this group at the last meeting, but I just want to say that your genuineness, your honesty, and the true caring I see in your hearts for your kids and your staff . . . well, you remind me why I have made the decision to return to the hot seat. I will be going back to the principalship this summer, and although I know it will be grueling at times, I can't wait." Linda looked toward John and smiled. "But, I'll need this group next year, so whoever makes out the e-mail list, count me in. And to John—thank you, sir, for unlocking the doors to our hearts, which makes all the difference in how we approach our jobs every day. Leading a school is impossible. Serving a school is a privilege."

Others followed, one by one, and John sat back and soaked it all in, realizing that he must not grow weary of the work he had been given to do. His goal was to give every principal in the state an opportunity to be a part of a support group like this. And as he stood to wrap up the session, he realized that there were people around this very table who were ready to facilitate cohorts of their own.

"Before we close," he said, "let's do one more thing. This time, as we go around the table, share a sentence or two that best describes what it means to be a servant leader in a school." He sat down, his pen ready to take notes, as he had realized that he always learned as much from his younger colleagues as they learned from him.

The principals in this group did not disappoint, as each offered his or her feeling about what it means to be a servant leader.

"Servant leading is mopping up in the boys bathroom if the custodian calls in sick or needs a hand that day."

"Serving leadership is caring enough to love the ones who get on your nerves just as much as the ones who appear to be the perfect employees."

"They all get on my nerves." Everyone cackled. John had to stop writing for a moment, he was laughing so hard.

"Serving is caring enough for the entire community that you lead with ethics and integrity, even when every now and then a harmless little shortcut seems to make so much sense."

"A servant leader does a whole lot of things you wouldn't normally want to do, because they need to be done. I've taken pies in the face, worn my pajamas to school, given speeches at graduations when I was so scared my knees almost buckled. I've checked heads for lice, and I've visited the hospital on Saturday mornings, and I've let staff and parents nail me to the wall of my office, all in the interest of finding the best solution to an issue. But if it made the school a little better and healthier place to be, then it was more than worth it."

"Servants are full of humility and show endless grace toward others."

"Leading from the heart means you apologize to that student, parent, or teacher you've offended, even if it takes you months or years to muster the courage to do so."

"Servant leadership is not about you. It's about them."

"Serving is waking up every morning, sometimes when you're so exhausted you can barely walk, and getting to school so the day runs smoothly for everyone else. They may not even realize they need you on most days.

But you being there, standing in the gap, allows the organization to grow and serve the community. It's like being a taxi driver, or a waitress, or an auto mechanic. People need you, so you keep doing it, day after day. It's your calling. It's your gift to humanity."

"A servant leader would give his or her life if the school was being taken apart by a tornado and even just one person was left inside helpless."

John closed with a final blessing as he looked into the eyes of everyone around the table. "A servant leader sees the good in everyone, and helps unlock the potential inside. Empowering and equipping is key. Preparing the organization to flourish after you leave is something you start working on your first day on the job. Servant leaders are wonderful, compassionate listeners, as you all have been with me this year. I have so enjoyed and learned from this group. It is an honor to call you all colleagues. It is an honor to call you friends."

In *Effective Succession Planning*, William J. Rothwell (2005) defines the concept of succession planning—preparing the organization to carry on seamlessly when the leader moves on. Succession planning is a key characteristic of servant leadership, as serving others includes empowering and equipping them to soar as leaders in their own right, free and strong.

Summary

John has an end-of-year cohort session, and the group shares from the heart what they are learning as they grow into mature servant leaders. One by one, they define what it means to be a leader of integrity who cares for other people. John is deeply moved, realizing he has been blessed to work with such a fine group of school leaders.

Reflection:

1. What support systems are the principals in your school district a part of?
2. What impact does the principal's leadership style have on the school's culture?
3. Is your principal a leader of leaders who empowers and equips others so the organization has an abundance of capacity?

CHAPTER TWENTY-FOUR

~

Shannon's Tribute

Life cannot be measured by length, acquisitions, wealth, fame, performance, or position. Life is measured by our relationships.

John was packing his truck, getting ready for a Saturday outdoors with his family, when the call came. Shannon Watson had passed away quietly in her sleep the night before. Brad had asked the family if he could read the tribute she had left as part of Smith School's graduation service the following Friday. He also hoped John would say something about what a student like Shannon means to a school community.

"I'll be there."

"Thank you, John." Brad's voice quivered as he hung up the phone.

John and his family arrived for graduation night an hour early so that he could make sure he was seated where Brad needed him. When he was introduced and he stood up, his knees buckled and he had to stand still for a moment to regain his coordination. Suddenly, his eyes seemed to make contact with every parent in the audience, and he was overwhelmed with the reality of life and death, and of being a father, and of how fast the early years slip away—when the kids are small, and every day is full of the hustle and bustle of family and all the emotion that goes with it. John put his notes back in his pocket, what he now felt led to say was completely spontaneous and unrehearsed.

"I have been asked to share a few words regarding what Shannon meant to this school. Simply put, the one time I had the privilege to meet her, she had such impact on me, I have had a renewed purpose for the work I do in school improvement ever since.

"You see, Shannon's life, and the way she lived it, reminds us why it is so important to not just do school, but embrace it and make it everything it can possibly be for every child, every day. And where does that begin? School is not an isolated place we send our kids to as some dreaded rite of passage into the next stage of life. School begins at home, and if we adults can figure it out, it is simply a beautiful extension of that home. Shannon lived in a loving home. And thus, in that home, she was already taught so, so much about how to celebrate life, and her family, and her friends, and her many talents. So coming to school every morning was as natural for her as playing and working around the house.

"And wasn't she a joy here at school? Didn't she make an impact? And wasn't her attitude during her illness a reminder to all of us about how living well is so much more than frantic schedules, endless tasks, rushing here and there but missing the very essence of life? Shannon reminded all of us that we are on a journey, a journey that is to be embraced, savored, cherished—every little part of it. Her model for how to honor home and school and relationship is a lesson that can further change this community."

John looked out across the large crowd, and he felt a deep kindred spirit for the people of Smithtown. "I have watched you this year transform this school into something special, closer to the original concept of school—an extension of home, like the community 'mom and pop' grocery store, like the community church. You have something magical going on here, folks. Let Shannon's example help you seize the opportunity even more eagerly. Embrace the potential of this school for all of your children, and for your precious community."

Shannon's family stood, and within moments, all in attendance joined them in an ovation that seemed to say, "We accept your challenge, and we will do it!"

Brad was next, as he stepped forward, he was wiping tears from his eyes. "I will need help getting through this letter Shannon wanted me to share with you all. So, as I read, please say a quiet prayer for me, folks." He put on his glasses, laid Shannon's pages in front of him, gripped both sides of the pulpit with his hands, and began:

Dear Smith School Family:
  By the time this gets read to you, I will have gone home to a better place. My body is weak, and I am tired. I am at total peace with dying, as I have accepted the reality of the brevity of life, and that we all only have a short time here. But I wanted to have one last opportunity to say 'thank you' to all of those

who have made my life so, so special. And by the way, thank you to Mr. Williamson, our principal, for reading this. He is a good man, and I am honored that he is doing this for me today.

First of all, thank you to Mom and Dad and my brothers and sister for providing for me a loving home. Mom and Dad, you taught me from the very beginning that I could do anything, and that I should chase my dreams. I have, and I only wish that I had more time to enjoy the blessings of being raised by such loving parents. Thank you for a safe and sheltered home, with laughter, and books, and hot breakfasts, and Saturday walks in the park, and pets, and a bicycle, and plenty of time at Mamaw and Papaw's house.

My siblings, who are also my best friends—Charlie, Bobby, and Melissa—you have a very important job to do in keeping our family strong. Be there for each other, and be there for Mom and Dad. Nothing can replace the love of family. Don't ever forget that or take it for granted.

Next, to my teachers: Thank you for believing in me and making school such a wonderful place to go to every morning. I especially remember the times you would talk to me about how my life was going, and ask me about my hobbies, or how my family was doing.

And when you read to us, or read to the class something I had written, when you changed the usual format so we were exploring and learning in new ways, when you let us create, when you turned us loose with our computers and used them in class with us, when you stayed after school to help us learn our parts to a play, when you were graceful—in control but gentle and respectful to us, when you laughed, or cried, and let us see the real you, when you took us to the state capitol, and played volleyball with us in the gym . . . and when you slowed down and patiently taught us something again if we didn't grasp it the first time—thank you.

And I must not forget the Smithtown community. This year, when our school burned, we kids worried that we may not have a school anymore. But you pitched in, and to be honest, this has been the best school year we've ever had! I loved it when the grownups would come in and tell us about their interesting lives and careers, or go with us on field trips, or invite us to help on a project out in the community, or come in and volunteer to tutor us, or read with us, or help our teachers with the extra work that often takes them away from what they love to do—teach.

And finally, thank you to my classmates, my family away from home. Guys, this is it. How fast these years have gone! I cherish the memories of learning and growing with you. I am laughing as I think back to the silly jokes at lunch, the games and sweating at PE and recess, the challenge of learning to play an instrument in band, the annual spring chorale festival.

Oh, I could go on and on! But, just remember, these were the times of our young lives. Your parents, your teachers, your principals, the whole community—they are there to be your foundation as you get this one chance to do your best with the talents God has given you, to live this life . . . prepared to make a difference . . . prepared to soar. So, go for it! Don't look down, don't look back, don't look beside you, don't look too far ahead and wish your life away. Just go for it. *Carpe diem!* Seize the day!

> I love you all,
> Shannon

Brad was able to finish reading, but then he broke into a long, soft cry as he stood in front of Smith School . . . Smith School, the people . . . Smith School, the community . . . Smith School, the relationships . . . Smith School, the memories . . . Smith School, the future . . . Smith School, his life.

As John sat with his family, tears streaming down his face, and looked over the crowd of grieving people who so deeply loved each other, an epiphany overwhelmed him. He smiled as he realized, "This is what we have all been looking for for so long. Just maybe we are not at the end of our journey. Maybe we are only at a bend in the road. Perhaps the bend leads to a better place, the road less traveled, the road we have so longed for—the road to relationship and the celebration of learning, and life, and truth . . . the road that leads back home."

In *Long Journey Home*, Os Guinness (2001) reflects on man's deepest questions about the meaning of life—and the universal truth that it is about so much more than ourselves.

Summary

Brad's student who is terminally ill, Shannon, passes away. She leaves a letter that she wanted shared with the Smithtown community, and Brad reads it at the high school graduation. Shannon's message not only soothes and heals, but shines light on the path to Smith School's future.

Reflection:

1. What lessons do we learn from the letter Shannon left for her school community?
2. Does your school community laugh and cry together? Is the school family healthy and strong or toxic and dysfunctional?
3. Do you measure your school's success by external rewards or in internal relationships and students fulfilling their potential?

~

CHAPTER TWENTY-FIVE

Closing Thoughts:
Unchained (The Space in Between)

Learning and the thirst for knowledge is as natural for a child as breathing. So, it stands to reason, when a school structure is complicated and uninspiring—there is a better way.

As early summer brought with it some time to get away for a few weeks, Brad kept getting requests from other educators around the country to come and see for themselves this small school that seemed to have so little, yet in reality had so much. Brad was working on a protocol for fall semester visits when John dropped in for a final chat.

"John, it's amazing. People want to borrow from our model. Who would have thought this would be possible last August on that fateful weekend of the fire?"

"Borrow from your model? Brad, they want to learn about and use your model—all of it. I am so proud of you. You and your school family here have figured it out."

"It seems so simple now, John. But tell me, how did we reinvent in such a short time? And what lessons are learned from this? It's as if we threw conventional wisdom out the window and came up with a recipe that is so superior to our old school, it's not even funny."

"And that's the key, Brad. Conventional, traditional, stereotypical—all words to describe an organization in danger of becoming stale and obsolete. We humans are drawn to status quo by nature. But visionaries, those who sense there's a better way, those who serve others by removing barriers—all have a disdain for 'business as usual.' So the fire, in a way, forced us to break out of the mode that was so trapping us into thinking convergently year after year. It freed us up to think divergently."

"Yes, and in the process, a much better teaching and learning model was born, a model that is focused every day on the core values of a true community learning center."

"So, what do you like best about the new and improved Smithtown School, John?"

"I love your attention to simplicity, Brad. I love the emphasis on the whole child. Your relentless refusal to allow students to slip through the cracks without being able to read and do math well is the cornerstone for every other course you teach. The life skills class and advisor-advisee provides a tremendous support system for your students that was not there before. And the coordination of community volunteers as a major human resource changes the dynamic of the student/teacher ratio completely."

John barely stopped to take a breath. He just kept reeling off examples. "The rethinking of time is a huge piece of your formula here, too. The four-day instructional week allows a monumental increase in parent conferences, plus extra clubs and field trips for the kids; rethinking how to use technology and online learning, and common planning time for your teachers to discuss student achievement and then make adjustments—again, these are huge paradigm shifts that make so much sense."

"And John, the teachers and the students, and their parents too, appreciate these new tools we've built into the total menu of services. I've never been around a place that just seems to be almost giddy all the time about the daily routine, the freshness of it all."

"Brad, what you just described is key. Schools for too long have been so preoccupied with the correctness, with being complex, hierarchical systems that seem to do everything but protect the sacredness of the relationship between mentor and the pupil. With the fire, the Smith School culture was forced to break free from those chains."

"And as we began to realize this freedom, it permeated the classrooms, too, John. Our students love their classes because our teachers have gone back to why they first decided to go into education. The emphasis on experiencing as we learn, and the freedom to leave behind the reliance on lecture and prescribed learning, has transformed how we're approaching lesson planning."

"Plus, John, the increase in the use of instructional technology has the kids so excited, and the celebration of their unique creative skills, hobbies, their private interests—what a shot in the arm these new approaches have been. Students engaged and loving coming to school—what a novel thought!"

"Indeed. What a novel thought!"

"How did we let it get so complicated, John?"

"The same way other large organizational structures in our society have become so dysfunctional, Brad—by spending way too much time on top down control and the creation of endless regulations that are too numerous to enforce and too impractical to be embraced by those in the grassroots who actually run the organization."

"John, I think I agree, but I couldn't repeat that to my wife if I had to!"

John laughed, and tried again. "Okay. Simply put, Brad, if largeness eliminates authenticity . . . if becoming sophisticated is detrimental to relationship . . . if control dissolves the community, you've got problems and it's not worth it. All the brick and mortar in the world, all the membership in this organization and that organization, all the national conferences you can possibly go to cannot transform a school that has become smothered in a crippled structure that does not realize it is broken."

"You're still going to have to make it simpler for me, John."

"In other words, Brad, teaching and learning is not complicated. How complicated is it for a mentor who truly cares for a pupil to help that pupil explore the vastness of his or her mind and of the world around them?"

"Perhaps it's such a natural process, it can't be prepackaged?"

"Yes! Exactly. And perhaps it's a process that requires, first and foremost, before anything else, the sincere care of the other person. So, teaching is relationship. Leading a classroom or leading a school is serving and connecting all available resources to the needs of the student."

"But isn't that what we've been doing all along, John? I don't know of anyone in education who doesn't try to provide a quality learning experience for the children they work with. And I don't have any principal buddies who aren't doing their best every day to build a great school."

"The effort's not the issue, Brad. And yes, most schools are full of dedicated adults who want what's best for their students. And make no mistake; many, many schools have innovative programs in place and can show data that indicates student achievement is doing okay. But too often, we allow a toxic culture of scattered agendas and a vague vision to permeate the day-to-day flow of the school. The classrooms are obviously affected. After a while, the reality is that the tail starts wagging the dog."

"How do you mean?"

"Well, as an example, I have worked with one school this year that allows its sports program to have way too much influence on other, seemingly unrelated facets of the total menu of student services. Another district I have worked with this year wants desperately to make major changes in its daily and weekly master schedule, but the bus schedule is so rigid, it is actually holding up a major school improvement initiative."

John ran his fingers through his hair as he thought of the many situations he had observed where the school structure and culture was not healthy, but there seemed to be no plan to change. "And a third example I can think of is a school a few miles away that is struggling to keep its student attendance up. More and more parents in the community are transporting their kids to neighboring districts that provide more learning opportunities. Is this school reinventing itself as your school chose to do? No. Too many adult powerbrokers on the staff and in the community have run things for so long, they'll go down with the ship rather than change."

"It's sort of like what my papaw told me, John, when he bought his first riding lawn mower. I will never forget it. We were sipping lemonade on his front porch, after working all morning down at his barn." Brad grinned as he thought of his papaw. "He had hired me that summer to come by and do chores and mow his grass. He sat back, wiped his forehead with a handkerchief, and said, 'Bradley, you know why I put my old push mower in the shed and broke down and bought me a riding lawn mower last summer?' I said, 'No, why, Papaw?' 'Because although I love the old mower, the newer one makes me smarter. It saves time. It saves my back and knees. Simply put, it's a better way to cut my grass. Why would I not use a better system? If I didn't, you could make a pretty good argument that my elevator didn't go to the top floor!'"

"So you're saying, Brad, that just maybe we in education are still using the push mower when there's a better way?"

"I'm just saying that this year, at Smithtown School, teaching was fun again. We had time. We had all the human resources we needed. We let go of all that stuff that had been bogging us down and engaged the kids in authentic relationships and relevant learning. I would never go back to the old system. Never."

"All because of a Friday night fire."

"All because we came up for air, looked around, and became a true community school again."

"I'm curious, Brad. What would be your five nonnegotiables? The five core values that you feel would be the key foundation for other schools that might want to use your model?"

Brad thought hard about John's question. "I'd start with sitting down with staff and fleshing out what their preferred future would look like if they could rethink their classrooms. Then I'd work with the staff to help them understand the relationship factor—trusting, healthy relationship with students, relationship with each other, relationship with parents, relationship with community.

"Next, I'd open the doors and invite the community in to help in any way they could—from one-on-one tutoring, to using the school's space for their needs, to helping with any other manpower gaps. And then I'd empower and equip everyone in the school community, including students, to explore what instructional technology really means in the 21st century. And lastly, I'd do away with anything that impeded the success of those first four core values."

"So, your top five would be: (1) unchained, innovative classrooms; (2) a relentless focus on healthy relationships; (3) partnership with the community integrated fully into the school culture; (4) expanded use of technology as a major instructional tool within and outside the classroom; and (5) elimination of anything else that might creep in to divide and scatter the commitment to these four drivers.

"I like your top five, Brad. But I don't see some of the traditional sacred cows on your list. In fact, you've left out some that cost bunches of money and that we have assumed for years a school could not do without."

"You're right. But guess what, John? We learned this year that what we needed were the essentials. All that stuff on the fringe that creeps into the fray to the point that we're taking care of everything but the most important—I would advise any principal, any school council, any superintendent, any school board to get out of the big business trap and keep it simple. Like you pointed out, what is it that summer camp has that motivates kids to want to go back again and again? What is it that causes school to be boring, and even dreaded, by some kids as early as third grade?" Brad gritted his teeth with disgust. "Whatever that artificial, adult-centered nonsense is, I simply say, 'Run as fast as you can from that stuff. It will suck the synergy and magic right out of your school!'"

"May I add three questions, Brad, that I think would add to your list of nonnegotiables?"

"Sure thing—shoot."

"First of all, why is there a school in the community? Next, how is it to serve? And finally, what must not be left out? If a small group of caring leaders can answer those questions, then they will know what to do in offering a high-quality school—whether for fifteen students, or a hundred, or a thousand."

"And nothing's stopping that community from rethinking its available space, its time, its human resources."

"Absolutely not—nothing at all—unless of course they like living in the caves, away from the light."

"Or using a push mower."

John slapped his knee and headed toward the door laughing. "See you this fall, Brad. I need you in that cohort again, unless of course you'd like to be the team leader for one of the new ones we're starting."

"Interesting idea. Let me think about it."

In *Positive Turbulence*, Stanley S. Gryskiewicz (1999) illustrates how leadership can develop climates for creativity, innovation, and renewal by bringing tension to the status quo and established order.

Summary

Brad asks John to share what he likes most about the new Smith School, and John in turn asks Brad to list his five "nonnegotiables," the core values that must remain a part of this new school model. Both agree that the reinvented Smith School, with its focus on relationship, serving, and empowerment of all human resources, is a better way.

Reflection:

1. What are three to five nonnegotiable core values of your school?
2. What conditions, control, or habits are detracting from these core values?
3. When are you going to eliminate these distractions from your school culture?

References

Bennett, W. J. 1999. *The index of leading cultural indicators: American society at the end of the twentieth century*. New York: Broadway Books.

Blanchard, K. 2007. *Leading at a higher level*. Upper Saddle River, NJ: Prentice Hall.

Christian, C., and R. Wallace. 2009. *Heart to heart: Awakenings*. Lexington, KY: Kentucky Cohesive Leadership System.

Davis, S. M. 1987. *Future perfect*. New York: Addison-Wesley.

Fullan, M. 2001. *Leading in a culture of change*. San Francisco, CA: Jossey-Bass.

Gardner, H. 2006. *Five minds for the future*. Boston: Harvard Business School Press.

Glaser, J. E. 2007. *Creating we*. Avon, MA: Platinum Press.

Green, R. L. 2009. *The four dimensions of principal leadership: A framework for leading 21st-century schools*. Boston: Allyn & Bacon.

Gryskiewicz, S. S. 1999. *Positive turbulence*. San Francisco, CA: Jossey-Bass.

Guinness, O. 2001. *Long journey home*. Colorado Springs, CO: Waterbrook Press.

Harvard Business School Press. 2006. *Coaching people: Expert solutions to everyday challenges*. Boston: Harvard Business School Press.

Harvard Business School Press. 2007. *Giving feedback: Expert solutions to everyday challenges*. Boston: Harvard Business School Press.

Kohn, A. 1999. *The schools our children deserve*. New York: Houghton Mifflin.

Maslach, C., and M. P. Leiter. 1997. *The truth about burnout*. San Francisco, CA: Jossey-Bass.

Maxwell, J. C. 2003. *Thinking for a change*. New York: Warner Books.

McKeever, B. 2003. *Nine lessons of successful school leadership teams*. San Francisco, CA: WestEd.

Michalko, M. 1991. *Thinkertoys*. Berkeley, CA: Ten Speed Press.

Palmer, P. J. 2007. *The courage to teach*. San Francisco, CA: John Wiley & Sons.

Palmer, P. J. 1993. *To know as we are known*. New York: HarperOne.

Peterson, K. D., and T. E. Deal. 2002. *The shaping school culture fieldbook*. San Francisco, CA: Jossey-Bass.

Rothwell, W. J. 2005. *Effective succession planning*. New York: Amacom.

Schwartz, P. 1996. *The art of the long view*. New York: Currency.

Sergiovanni, T. J. 2005. *Strengthening the heartbeat*. San Francisco, CA: Jossey-Bass.

Taleb, N. N. 2007. *The black swan: The impact of the highly improbable*. New York: Random House.

Zemelman, S., H. Daniels, and A. Hyde. 1998. *Best practice: New standards for teaching and learning in America's schools*. Portsmouth, NH: Heinemann.

~

About the Author

Rocky Wallace teaches graduate classes in instructional leadership and writes leadership curriculum as a full-time faculty member at Morehead State University. As a former principal, he writes his articles and books from the unique perspective of the practitioner down in the trenches. This book is his third in a series published by Rowman & Littlefield Education on the role the principal plays in school improvement.

While Wallace was principal at Catlettsburg Elementary in Boyd County, Kentucky, the school was named a Kentucky and U.S. Blue Ribbon School in 1996–1997. He began his administrative career while serving as principal at Fallsburg School, a P–8 center in Lawrence County, Kentucky (his home county, where he was born and raised).

As he moved on to leadership consulting work with the Kentucky Department of Education in 2000, and later as Director of Instructional Support at the Kentucky Educational Development Corporation in Ashland, Kentucky, Wallace realized that school principals of this generation face a perplexing dilemma: they are being asked to do more and more in turning our nation's educational system around, but too often without the needed support of caring and experienced mentors who have been principals themselves.

While studying strategic leadership as he completed his doctoral work at Regent University in Virginia Beach, Virginia, Wallace realized that the answer in how to create more effective schools that focus on the holistic needs of children and youth is in embracing the principles of servant leadership.

Thus, the core values of "serving" and putting people over profit, while addressing key organizational culture issues, is found throughout his writing.

Wallace received his undergraduate degree from Berea College in 1979, and MA from Morehead State in 1983. He is married to Denise, who is the director of Calvary Christian School, located near Catlettsburg. The couple have two teenage daughters, Lauren and Bethany, and live on a small farm. In his spare time, Wallace pastors a small United Methodist church, Whites Creek, and volunteers at Calvary. He also provides consulting support to other education agencies, assisting in writing leadership curriculum. His hobbies include enjoying the outdoors and traveling with his family.